† CATHOLIC
† HOME LIBRARY

THE CHURCH TODAY:
BELONGING AND BELIEVING

ANTHONY T. PADOVANO

FC Books
Los Angeles

PRESIDENT:
Rev. Anthony Scannell, Capuchin

EDITORS:
Gary Bradley, MA; Robert Delaney, STD
Corinne Hart, PhD; Karl Holtsnider

SERIES CONSULTANTS:
Francis Colborn, STD
Rev. James Gehl, MA, M.Div.
Alexis Navarro, PhD

ART and PHOTOGRAPHY:
Art Director: Robert Miller
Graphic Assistance: Christine Soldenski,
Therese Denham, CSJ
Photo Editors: Lucy Liu Brown, MA
Staff Photographers: Michael McBlane
Ralph Swanson

EDITORIAL ASSISTANCE:
Peg Bradley; Elmer Carroll, SJ; Rose
Delaney; Loretta Hernandez; Christi
Montes; Elizabeth Montes; Rev. C.
Vincent Peterson, MA; Patricia Rocap,
BVM; Kevin Schroeder, OFM

MARKETING:
Direction/Research: William Sheck;
Jose Velasquez; Helen Payne
Assistance: Ida DeGeorge; Eloise Evans;
Blanca Gallegos; Dorla Lord; John
MacDonell, OFM; John Midkiff; Ann
Palacio; Patrice Russell; Rosita Steer
Adela Stewart; Yolanda Young

© 1990 Franciscan Communications

Library of Congress Catalog Card
Number: 88-82645
ISBN: 1-55944-001-5

COVER PHOTO:
Pope John Paul II's visit to Los Angeles.

Quotations from Scripture are adapted
from the **New American Bible,**
copyright ©1970, with revised New
Testament, copyright ©1986, by the
Confraternity of Christian Doctrine,
Washington, D.C., and are used with
permission.

Quotations from the Second Vatican
Council are adapted from **VATICAN
COUNCIL II, The Conciliar and Post
Conciliar Documents**, Two Volumes,
Austin Flannery, O.P., Gen. Editor;
Costello Publishing Co., Northport, N.Y.,
Revised Edition ©1988.

CATHOLIC HOME LIBRARY books
make available in an informative and
inspiring way the riches of church teaching and practice as they have developed
since the Second Vatican Council.

For more information please contact:
Franciscan Communications
1229 S. Santee Street
Los Angeles, CA 90015
(213) 746-2916 / (800) 421-8510

CONTENTS

I   Origins: A Cosmic Vision

1 New Wine   9

2 Bread for the World   19

3 Spirit and Memory   29

4 Word and Scripture   41

II   Visions: Hope and Commitment

5 Symbols and Sacraments   55

6 Authority and Conscience   67

7 Ministry and Service   77

8 Parish and Community   89

III Enduring Questions: Continuing Challenges

9 Catholic Identity   103

10 Fidelity and Destiny   113

List of the Popes   122

Glossary/Index   124

I. ORIGINS: A COSMIC VISION

1

New Wine

It once began with a man and a woman. But then the relationship was different, and the origins of it all were lost somewhere between myth and history. The story is a fascinating one and so we continue to tell it, less sure of its particulars than we are of its meaning.

The Genesis story of the beginnings of human life still works for us today because it is as mysterious and assertive as our own existence. There is a sense in all of us that more than the resources of this planet were

"They went astray in the desert wilderness.... their life was wasting away.... God sent his Word to heal them and to snatch them from destruction" (cf. Psalm 107:4,19-20).

When we tell the stories of the first man and the first woman, they are not stories of them as much as they are stories of us. They are stories, furthermore, of the nature of the universe and of the character of the God responsible for it.

Genesis centers its human meaning in the relationship of a man and a woman and in their dialogue with the source of their life. A whole universe is compressed, so to speak, in the love of two people for each other, in a man and a woman, in their marriage and mutual experience, in their fear and fidelity, in their permanent and sometimes troubled relationship.

It is no wonder that the creation story enchants us. It moves from whirling suns and planets, from massive oceans and rivers, from the canopy of heavens and distant horizons, from life in all its myriad forms, to a garden where a man and a woman meet and name each other and discover between them a force which explains and justifies the mighty drama of life. The glory of a created universe is no more captivating than the grandeur of the human relationship itself. The script of the cosmos is lettered with love as its first word.

It begins with a man and a woman because these are the basic ingredients of marital love. They are also the fundamental elements of life. In a man and a woman, love is given a face and a name; life is endowed with a human body and a human heart. A new architecture for meaning is created as the cosmos encounters itself and God in the form of a creature.

Creation achieves humanity in the making of a man and a woman. This humanity is rooted in the earth from which the first man is molded and in

required to bring human life into being. Scientifically, we affirm that the entire cosmos, from stars to atoms, conspired in our conception. Theologically, we assert that a force more powerful and intelligent, more benign and free, more loving and personal was the ultimate cause of us.

In any case, we came into being. The emergence of such a phenomenon as ourselves is so awesome that the entire universe and an infinite God are not too much of a reference point to explain how we got here.

the bones and flesh of human life from which the first woman is fashioned. The result of all this is human beings, created in exquisite simplicity as well as in the complexity of a seemingly impossible design.

And so, we have human life and human persons. It began, as we noted, with a man and a woman. It always begins there.

A New Creation

The story of creation, the origins of the universe and the fate of the earth are the background for our reflection on the Church. The Church is not only in the world but of the world, in the sense that it derives from the world itself.

The marital love of man and woman, the family which emerges from them and the home life which is created by these relationships are at the heart of the Church. There can be no Church unless men and women bring it into being as surely as they bring human life into being. It is not as though men and women create Church or children with no reference to the divine, solely on their own resources, as it were. Rather, it is God who allows neither Church nor children to exist without reference to marital life and love.

The Church, too, begins with a man and a woman. This is true not only in the instance of marital love but also on another level.

The key relationship of man and woman is, for the Church, a different relationship. It is not husband and wife but mother and son at the heart of the Church's origins.

The family model used by the authors of Genesis for the story of the universe becomes the model used by the New Testament writers for the story of the Church. The family model, in this instance, is not essentially marital but parental and maternal. The man and woman are not the Adam and Eve whose bones and flesh are fused into one life. The man and woman are now Jesus and Mary whose spirit and sinlessness are shared. Jesus is also flesh of Mary's flesh and bone of her bone. But the sense of the passage is different. The evangelists see the origins of Jesus as a renewal of the story of creation but all this is now done in a different key.

Adam and Eve are called into being by the Word of God; Mary and Jesus are summoned into existence by the Spirit of God. Mary conceives by the Spirit, and Jesus is the Spirit's finest creation. Adam and Eve never lost the image of God in which they were

In Jesus' victory over death, the desert is overcome in a new way and the waters of life flow once more.

The Church takes Jesus from the arms of Mary to care for him, but quickly discovers that the child who is received is the child who leads.

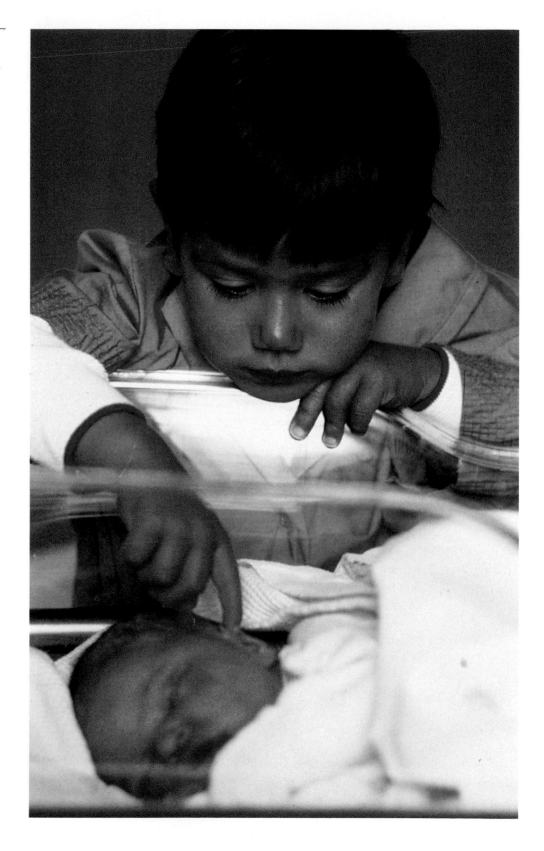

made, but fidelity for them, as well as for us, is a commitment tarnished by human weakness. Jesus and Mary, made in God's image, are faithful to the uttermost so that humanity will not lack the full measure of its greatness.

If the story of creation is one of the most compelling stories ever told, the story of Christmas is one of the most moving narratives ever written. It too has in it the cosmic sweep of the creation account. There are stars to follow and deserts to cross, celestial music and angelic visitors, dreams from another world and prophecies fulfilled in this one.

In the background, there is a saga of passion and fidelity as Mary and Joseph begin a marital relationship together. In the foreground, there is a parable of maternal love and religious fervor as a young Jewish woman makes the miracle of conception all the more marvelous by the interaction of the human and the divine in the creation of a child.

Woman is made from man at the beginning of creation; man is made from woman at the beginning of Christian history. The Word which conceives creation is now conceived. Eve was flesh of Adam's flesh; Jesus was bone of Mary's bone. In all these reversals, there is continuity and completion.

This story too is simple in the telling but complex in its significance. Once again, the meaning of human life depends upon the relationship of a man and a woman.

The New Adam

Jesus is the center of the Church's concern even though a church was not at the center of his preaching. The

Human beings are created in exquisite simplicity as well in the complexity of a seemingly impossible design.

Church is interested in every detail of the life of Jesus even though Jesus gives us few, if any, details about the Church. And, yet, in spite of this, Jesus and Church are forever linked in history.

Jesus remains active in human history through those who love and believe in him, namely, the Church. Indeed, both the New Testament and later Christian tradition believe that the relationship between Christ and the Church is fittingly presented by comparing it to the relationship of husband and wife. In this comparison, the Church is the spouse of Christ. Once again, we are involved with the image of man and woman, with a marital and a family model in the presentation of our theology.

No one knows exactly what it was that led Jesus out of Nazareth to a life of preaching and mission, of miracle and sacrifice. Something happened to this young man on the banks of the River Jordan near the end of the third decade of his life. He and John the Baptist met and Jesus was baptized. The Baptism became for Jesus a

"Yet, God, in your great mercy you did not forsake your people in the desert. The column of cloud did not cease to lead them by day... nor did the column of fire by night..." (cf. Nehemiah 9:19).

moment of profound illumination, an interior enlightenment which convinced him that he was God's Son in a unique way and that this hour was a time for reform and that he himself was to be the reformer.

This story of vocation and obedience is a powerful narrative. It occurs somewhere between the River Jordan and the desert. The waters of Baptism and the sands of temptation mingle as Jesus encounters God and then confronts Satan.

Jesus goes into the desert after he emerges from the river just as Israel once went into the desert after coming up from the parted sea. Israel found, to its wonder, that the sea was opened up miraculously for it and that the desert was to become a fertile place where it would be tested and given a mission. Jesus discovers, to his astonishment, that the heavens are torn open miraculously as the Spirit urges him into the desert where he too will be tried and given a mission.

These continuing parallels between Christian history and Jewish life, between Israel and Jesus, are one of

the most artful and complex features of the Gospel tradition. Jesus is constantly presented as the mid-point between a past which he recapitulates as Israel's Messiah and a future which he heralds as the Church's Savior. All of this history and vision are encapsulated in one, brief life and on a level of intensity and symbol, of simplicity and parable that is breathtaking.

We alluded to the relationships between Christmas and Eden earlier in this chapter. We know now that Baptism and Exodus are also joined. At issue, in the life of Jesus, is not only the whole of Jewish and Christian history, but also our understanding of the divine and the human. It is no wonder that the Church has Jesus as its center and finds itself enthralled by him.

The young man emerges from the desert as a powerful preacher. His word seems to have a compelling force which reminds one of Genesis where the Word of God molds the physical structure of the cosmos and lifts it from chaos to life. Here, in Jesus, the Word of God reaches the spiritual core of the human family and transforms it from law to love. No religious leader in all human history spoke of God so intimately or identified God as love so forcefully.

A Law of Love

If Jesus' preaching tells us anything, it tells us first of all that God is primarily a parent and that law is a less desirable approach to divine life. It is not that law is unimportant; it is merely minimal.

The family model helps here once again. No husband and wife build their relationship on law if their marriage is successful, even though they may abide by rules of procedure. These rules are not nothing, but they are clearly marginal to their love experience and emerge from it. No parent and child define their bonding as

primarily legal if their relationship is sound, even though parents and children observe rituals of discipline and respect.

The choice Jesus makes for love over law is one of the most central themes in his preaching. The Christian community will forever after struggle with this delicate equation of trying to make love the substance of all Church life, so that the Church is truly the Church of Christ. Yet the Church is aware of the need Jesus had to follow the law even as he transformed it. Jesus is a reformer, not an anarchist. And so the Church senses a need for law and discipline, for order and procedure.

It would not be helpful for people who assemble to worship Christ and to serve the world to do anything they wished. And yet it is not proper for people who are made free by Christ to

JESUS AS CENTER

The central focus of the Church must always be on the life of Jesus. This is why the Church is most fully itself in those who are devoted disciples rather than in those who are office-holders.

This in no way invalidates the legitimate role office-holders play in the Church. It does, however, assert priorities. No one is asked to join the Church for the sake of holding office but rather for the sake of discipleship. Officers of the Church are impressive if they are, first of all, faithful followers of Christ.

The Christian community cherishes, over the centuries, those contemplatives and saints whose lives reflect Christ rather than office holders who had valid authority but little love. We remember Benedict and Francis of Assisi better than whoever was Pope during their lifetimes, whether those Popes were good men or not.

This is not to say that Popes and Bishops have not been at times impressive saints and faithful disciples. It is to say, however, that the central task of all Christians is the following of Christ and not the rank that one has in the community.

"In the beginning was the Word, and the Word was with God, and the Word was God.... and this life was the light of the human race" (John 1:1,3).

be told all or even most of the things they must do by law before they can be accepted as full members of the Church. Law is always incidental to a healthy life even though it is constructive on its own terms and in its own time.

It is ironic that the man of love over law should have been brought to death by the law. It is as though the law,

confronted with its adversary, made a mighty effort to destroy someone who would define God less as a law-maker and essentially as a love-giver.

In the horror of the cross, love prevails even as all the details of legal execution are observed. In this final drama, Jesus gives an example with his flesh and blood of the teaching he once declared in word and spirit.

The last scene in the life of Jesus is filled with trust and terror. Bread is broken in memory and affection before the departure; wine and the washing of feet are shared in gestures of farewell. The trial is a synthesis of fidelity and witness by Jesus, of abandonment and betrayal by the disciples. And, then, the cross is raised into the consciousness of all later world history, bearing on it the broken Body of Christ who a short time before had been baptized for the salvation of Israel and the world.

The man Jesus dies as the woman Mary watches. It is a man and a woman again, at the end as at the beginning. In the arms of Mary, Jesus becomes a child who belongs to all of us. Once before, he was ours as a child when she held him for the first time in the Christmas story; as she holds him for the last time, he is even more ours because it is we who must now care for him. We become his mother and father, his brothers and sisters. The Church takes Jesus from the arms of Mary to care for him but discovers that the child who is received is the child who leads us.

Jesus is an object of love as God's Son and our child, as Mary's first born and our brother, as spouse of the Church and Lord of history. There is more richness and depth to such a life than all history can exhaust.

Easter is the Christmas moment for Christ's Church.

And so, the Church will come into being slowly, but not as an organization founded by Jesus in all its structural parts. That would be too easy and superficial. The Church begins as a community so captivated by Christ that it will need all its history to meditate about him. This meditation will lead to contemplation and action.

The story of the Church begins with a man and a woman. The Spirit which compelled the creation of Jesus in the womb of Mary urges Christ out of the tomb. The God of love over law is vindicated by this victory over death. The desert is now overcome in a new way and the waters of life flow once more. Jesus brings bread out of the wilderness of the grave and offers the wine of a new heaven and a new earth for all God's children.

The joy of the Church has never been able to contain all the exuberance with which it learns that the tomb is empty and our hearts are full. The Easter experience creates not only a new life for Jesus but a new community for us. The Church does not trace its origins to its having been given a law or a plan but to its experience of life in the face of death. The Easter experience leads the disciples to break bread again, with all the tragic memories of cross and tomb evoked by that, but also to believe that Jesus is present triumphantly in his glory and that his Spirit baptizes us for mission.

Easter is not only a feast of Jesus. It is also the birthday of the Church. Easter is the Christmas moment for the Church of Christ.

2

BREAD FOR THE WORLD

Jesus had hardly arrived when it was time for him to go. There is no accurate way of knowing how long a time passed from the baptism in the Jordan to the Easter apparitions in Jerusalem. It may have been a year. Even if it were as long as three years, the longest possible time span, it was short-lived.

There is no way of knowing why it had to be so brief. Was the life of Jesus like a poem or a song which must be accomplished quickly so that the essence of the meaning might endure? A poet seeks beauty in words

(photo right)
"Teach me, O Lord,
your path that I may
walk in your truth..."
(Psalm 86:11).

which are the fragmentary remnants of an elusive wholeness. Was this why the life of Jesus was succinct?

The words of Jesus evoke rather than grasp God; and so, more of them might have told us less. The time Jesus was with us, no matter how long, would always have been a partial revelation of God and Christ's own fullness of life. So, further years might have been unnecessary. All insight is timeless. More parables and miracles, more years and encounters, might have been superfluous.

When a moving poem is over, one wishes it were not and yet knows that it had to be. Jesus departs from us with desire left in us for more of him. Just as a poem goes on in our memory of it, so Jesus is not absent as long as there are memories to hold him. Just as a poem takes on new meaning in the very absence of further words, so Jesus is revealed more when the seeing of him has passed.

There are many reasons, no doubt, to justify the brevity, but they do not make the passing less poignant or the absence less disappointing.

The disciples lost Jesus. It was as simple and painful as that. The loss did not only culminate in the tragic anguish of the cross. The final farewell, in Easter glory, was joyful and triumphant. But it was a farewell, nonetheless.

Now, there were only memories, the residue of a presence that seemed no longer available, the echo of a voice no longer heard, the footfalls of a journey not yet complete.

The memory of the night before Jesus died became the memory most easily reenacted. It was a memory replete with profound meaning, with mystery and sacramental significance.

The memory of that night included the recollection of those years which preceded it. Christmas and the Passover they had shared together were in the final Breaking of the Bread that night.

In the Last Supper memory, the disciples recalled the first time Jesus summoned them and the wonder with which they beheld the miracles and listened to the parables. The memory included the prayers they prayed with Jesus and the questions they asked him, the doubts which assaulted them and the faith which grew stronger as they spent time with Jesus. They remembered the washing of their feet and the tender words of friendship and farewell around the table of fellowship. It all seemed to be there as they broke bread and shared wine, reenacting what they could not wholly recover.

The memory of that night included also the events which immediately transpired after it. The crucifixion was in the breaking of bread, and the Easter experiences in the pouring of wine. They remembered the Bread given them as proof of forgiveness by the Risen Christ, the breakfast on the shores of Galilee, the promise of peace and everlasting presence, the fires of Pentecost.

The disciples broke bread with all this in mind and in faithfulness to the request of Jesus that whenever they would do this they might remember him.

One Bread, One Body

The Church took on a different shape and form as the disciples broke bread after Jesus was gone. In a sense, the Church began in those celebrations and shared experiences.

We say this for two reasons. In the first place, the Breaking of the Bread assembled the disciples as a community. It gathered them in a new and unique manner. They were alone now. Jesus was physically gone. They gained courage and strength as they repeated the very actions of Jesus and somehow made them their own. They repeated his words, giving them new meaning and sensing his presence as they did this. They needed one another to sort this out and ask whether it was Christ they encountered or only their own desperate need to have him present. They eventually realized it was both. But since the Breaking of the Bread was crucial to all this, it took on a significance for them they had not anticipated.

There was a level of intimacy here and of identity with Jesus that nothing else could match. In this action, they came to comprehend how they were the Body of Christ, member for member.

If they were the Body of Christ, then they could receive the Holy Spirit

Jesus is not absent as long as there are memories to hold him.

as the Body of Jesus once did in the womb of Mary, at the baptism in the Jordan, and in the tomb of Calvary. The Spirit was linked with the Body of Christ. Since they were now the Body of Christ, they too were inseparable from God's Spirit.

This Spirit, inflaming them with a desire for mission and enlightenment at Pentecost, would not only assemble them around the table but inspire them for mission. The Spirit would make them a community formed by contemplative memories, but also a people of word and witness. The bread in the hands of the early disciples was not only bread for those who were the Body of Christ but bread for the world as well.

Another reason why the Breaking of Bread began the Church in a special way was the sense of equality it fostered. This was to be not only a community in Christ but a community for one another.

There is something wonderful and perilous in the sharing of meals. The wonder is in the joy and the companionship, in the festivity and the bonding. The peril is in the degree of sacrifice for one another implicit in such an act of intimacy. A community gathered for nourishment not only gains life from the bread it shares, but gives its life for the sake of those who need life. If a member suffers, all are wounded. If a member rejoices, all are renewed.

This sense of equality helped the early disciples to define themselves with a minimum of reference to authority. Ministry meant more than hierarchy, community more than conformity.

The disciples met in homes rather than synagogues. And they came to

the startling conclusion that they were neither slave nor free, neither Jew nor Gentile, neither male nor female in this assembly. They were all one in Christ; legal, ethnic and gender differences faded into insignificance.

The breaking of bread began the Church as a family, not as an institution or an ideology, not as a religion or a social body, but as a family.

There would, of course, be other tasks to accomplish. A family always has them. There would be, at later moments, questions of authority and mission to be addressed. There would be a belief system to formulate and a moral code, a biblical record to write and structures for proclamation and preaching, evangelization and catechesis.

All of this would happen properly, it was assumed, if the Church were believed in first of all as a family whose fundamental sign of life is gathering around the table of the Lord. This was the first memory of Church; it has always been the best. It has never been a complete memory but it endures as a key memory by which to

The breaking of bread began the Church as a family.

(photo left) "Great ideas, it has been said, come into the world as gently as doves....a faint flutter of wings, the gentle stirring of life and hope" (Albert Camus).

THE EUCHARIST AND THE GOSPELS

If one compares the Synoptic Gospels (Matthew, Mark, Luke) with the Gospel of John, one can see a difference in emphasis in the Eucharist, a difference we have touched on in this chapter. For the Synoptics, the Last Supper is seen as an action of Christ and the community. The description of the Supper is given with a strong stress on Passover and on ritual. The community is in the forefront of this depiction, a community invited to remember Christ in this fashion.

In John, the angle of perception differs. John does not portray the Last Supper in its ritual form. He does not speak of the bread and wine given to the disciples. Rather, he moves the scene to an earlier part of his Gospel when Jesus describes himself as bread for the world and nourishment for the human family. Here, the Eucharist is not only for the disciples, gathered as a community, but for all those who see and hear

Christ. Here, the Eucharist is not reenacted in the Upper Room but in a much broader sense in the world at large.

These two dimensions of the Eucharist, the ritual of the community and the symbol of its relationship to the world, will give rise to different emphases on the Eucharist in subsequent Christian history.

measure the Church. It makes a world of difference if one defines the Church primarily as an *institution* which calls families together, or as a *family* with some institutional structure. The character and quality of life depends upon the model one uses to organize it.

When the disciples gather then, for the first time after the departure of Jesus, to break bread, they hold in their hands not only Christ but the Church, not only the Lord but the disciples, not only the Risen Jesus but the Easter community, not only God's Anointed but God's family.

Easter Faith

Throughout this process of celebration and commemoration, the unifying theme was faith in the Easter Presence of the Lord. Easter, like so much of the life of Christ, was an experience of fragments and wholeness. It was fragmentary in its elusiveness and whole in its capacity to make all the other pieces in the puzzle of Christ's life fit together.

The disciples seemed to be less a part of Jesus in the Easter apparitions. His elusiveness was so bewildering that even they could not always be sure it was Jesus whom they were seeing. The Easter Christ is only accessible to those who believe in him; and belief is never easy to define. There are no words or deeds from Jesus to convince unbelievers. The disciples now had to invite people to a wild and almost unbelievable act of faith, a belief in a human being who shared the prerogatives of divinity and yet was a crucified Messiah, someone thoroughly Jewish and yet universal, someone who had died and was buried and came back to life!

To sustain their belief in all this, there were only fragments. There was an empty tomb; burial clothes had been left behind; there were fleeting en- counters with disciples who, after all, had a vested interest in seeing Christ vindicated. Like faith itself, Easter offered no hard evidence, only witnesses and their appeal to something in us which always remains vulnerable to faith.

Easter faith was put together from fragments and hints, from guesses and conjectures, until it became a whole faith, courageous and certain, baffling and yet convincing. The Easter faith of the disciples, like the Eucharist they celebrated, was an experience of seeing only parts of a reality that existed in its completion elsewhere. It was a frightening and exuberant moment.

If the disciples were wrong, they would forfeit their lives to an illusion. If they were right, who would believe them?

How could a religious system emerging from a belief in Easter ever become more than the conviction of a small, frightened, confused circle of believers? The early disciples were raised with a Jewish faith which was sophisticated and complex, enduring and resilient. To preach a Risen Christ

in such a context would make them liable to charges of simple-mindedness at the very least. Jewish faith tests and questions, challenges and critiques. How could an Easter proclamation withstand such scrutiny?

Yet, if the disciples did not affirm their Easter faith, the very Christ who had become the center of their lives would be betrayed once again by them and in an even worse manner. Fidelity to Christ now meant fidelity to Easter as well. If the disciples were right, then the most wonderful thing that would happen in all of human history had just occurred and they were summoned to be part of it, witnesses and even martyrs to a phenomenon

"Lord, accept the prayers and gifts we offer in faith and love" (The Mass: Prayer over the Gifts).

A person (Christ), a sacrament (Eucharist), and a creed (Easter) are at the heart of the Christian community.

which changed all their thinking and became the major reference point for their lives.

The assurance that all this was believable would be achieved in the Eucharistic gathering of the community. Here, too, fragments were somehow wholeness, not only in the broken bread but also in the different members of Christ's Body made complete in their gathering as a community of faith. Easter and Eucharist were, therefore, joined in an inseparable manner. Both were fragmentary experiences pieced together until they became total indications of Divine Presence. Both exceeded all the expectations of the disciples' faith, even in its most vibrant intensities. Nothing, in a sense, prepared the disciples for either occurrence.

The Eucharist became the sacrament of the community's Easter faith. Easter

became the guarantee that the Eucharist was indeed communion with the enduring life of Christ.

Thus, Easter and Eucharist were the basic experiences that formed the community and informed its faith. The Church was a reality made up of faith (Easter) and sacrament (Eucharist). These would become the cornerstones of the new temple to be built, a temple which would become not only the Church, the community of Christ, but the Body of Christ as well.

At the Last Supper, Jesus told the disciples that there were many things he had not told them which they were yet to learn. In Easter and Eucharist, this prophecy was fulfilled. At the Last Supper, Jesus told the disciples that the Spirit would now be the community's rabbi and teacher. In Easter and Eucharist, through the action of the Holy Spirit, this prophecy came to pass. Pentecost confirmed the Easter and Eucharistic faith of the disciples and commissioned them to be its messengers.

Christ, Eucharist, and Easter

In these first two chapters, we have touched on the three central realities in the life of the Church: Christ, Eucharist and Easter. In subsequent Christian history, there would never be a Christian community which did not define itself in reference to these three central beliefs.

Christian Churches would differ and divide but in these three points they would be agreed. A person (Christ), a sacrament (Eucharist) and a creed (Easter) are at the heart of Christian community.

"What will God say to us, if some of us go to him without the others?" (Charles Peguy)

There were moments in Christian history when the New Testament was not yet written and, perhaps, centuries before it was officially compiled as we know it today, and yet the community was able to live. This is not to say that the New Testament is not also at the heart and core of Christian community, especially for those centuries after which the Twelve have passed into history and the Bible becomes the only written form of apostolic witness and testimony.

When the New Testament is finally written and received by the Church, it functions as a written norm for subsequent Christian communities and as an intimate part of the Christ experience, the eucharistic celebration and Easter faith. In this writing, the Spirit, active in all three of these events, will be active once again.

The community encounters the Body of Christ in the trinity of these essential elements which make up the Church. In Christ, the Body of Jesus is physical and historical; in Eucharist, the Body of Jesus is sacramental and ecclesial; in Easter, the Body of Jesus is risen and glorified.

The Spirit is an intimate influence in the destiny of Christ's Body, from conception to resurrection. This Spirit now moves the community to put into writing a Scripture which becomes, in a sense, the verbal incarnation of Christ's presence and of the community's memory of him. In the New Testament, both the testimony of the apostles and the Spirit's witness to Christ are proclaimed. In subsequent centuries, Christians will test the validity of their faith in Christ, Eucharist and Easter by this written expression of it.

The new wine of Christ's life, which we alluded to in the first chapter, is complemented by the Bread of Christ's Body which has been the subject of this chapter. The Bread and Wine bring us the Easter faith and Presence which define the Church at its most fundamental level. The Bread the Church is given is not only Christ's Body but also the Church's Body. This Bread is meant not only for the disciples gathered as an Easter community, but for all those in the world in need of a faith not easily defined, a hope not readily exhausted, a love which exceeds all knowing.

3

SPIRIT AND MEMORY

I n the process of our growing as an individual person, there are certain key events
and experiences which have a determining
influence on us. They are not always easily
definable nor, indeed, are we always aware of
them.

We are shaped by the environment or
atmosphere in which we live, by the assumptions and values implicit in our milieu, by our
conscious decisions and their not always
obvious implications.

Perhaps we can be more concrete. When a child is born, a number of important factors are put in place, factors which are received by the person as an inheritance and which set the context of the person's life. These would include: the identity of one's parents, the genetic and gender determination of the individual, the moment in history and time in which one lives, the citizenship one has in a nation, the language one learns, the social and economic level of one's childhood. These are determined before one is born.

We can apply this thinking to our reflections on the Church for a moment. The Church inherits the three basic elements—Christ, Eucharist, Easter—which we surveyed in the preceding chapters. These factors are given to the Church. The Church had no decision nor even much influence

in their formulation. Christ, Eucharist and Easter bring the Church not only into being but into being in a certain manner.

Growth and Change

But like ourselves, the Church is also formed by influences that are more freely chosen. Each of us inherits some of the essential characteristics and contexts of our lives, as we have seen. There are, however, further influences on us, influences which our parents do not quite so immediately determine, influences which are not set and settled by the time, place and culture of our birth.

These influences are more in our control, more subject to our freedoms, more optional in terms of whether they need to occur or not. It is true that even these choices are shaped in some way by the prior conditions of our origins. Nonetheless, they are "ours" in a way that the inherited factors are not. The inherited factors are "ours" only in the sense that we accept them and work within them. This is quite different from decisions about our lives that we originate and carry out ourselves.

What might some of these decisions be? We determine, for example, a course of studies to pursue or a profession to follow, a particular person to marry and the number of children to nurture, the place where we choose to live and the way we shall relate to learning, music, money, public issues. These choices enter deeply into our identity. None of them can be predicted beforehand, not by one's parents nor even by one's self. These are decisions **we** make. They become the "tradition" of our life.

"Wisdom is a loving spirit" (cf. Wisdom 1:6).

We are suggesting that the Church, as it travels its pilgrim road through time, makes a number of crucial decisions. These decisions need not have gone the way they did. The path of the Church is not so set and determined by Christ that no freedom is left to it. When these decisions are made, they enter into the very character of the Church's life and cannot be easily changed.

To continue the example, we might add that a person sometimes changes a profession or enters into a second marriage. A person might develop different attitudes towards learning or money or where one ought to live. Such changes are not easy and they never become what we might call total changes. In the new path the person chooses to follow, the former profes-sion or the first marriage, the prior attitude toward learning or the earlier place of residence have entered profoundly into the person's life and are always, to an extent, present and influential.

So it is with the Church. What these ever-present decisions might be for the Church we have yet to discuss.

There is one final point to make before designating which particular decisions become abiding influences in the Church's life. This point concerns the distinction which must be made between substantive decisions and useful decisions.

Substantive decisions, for an individual, would include those key life choices we have cited above in our discussion. Useful decisions would involve choices which do not enter

God's Spirit saves the Church from its excesses just as the same Spirit makes the Church a marvel and a miracle to behold.

deeply into our consciousness and identity. Among these we might number the clothing we choose or the kind of automobile we purchase, the foods we prefer or the color scheme in our homes. These choices must be made. Yet, having made them, we realize that they possess an extrinsic,

disposable character. Indeed, if we give too much time or energy to them, we become obsessive and are often judged superficial. And yet the choices are not unimportant.

To apply this principle to the Church, we might place in this category of useful but not substantive

decisions the following: the language in which the Liturgy is celebrated, the procedure by which the Pope is elected, the organization of the Church into dioceses and parishes, laws of fast and abstinence, of celibacy and marriage. As we can see, these are items of no little moment. And yet all of them were once done differently in church history from the way they are done now. All of them might be changed in the future without anything substantial to the Church's life being essentially altered.

The process of continuity in our individual lives is mysterious and difficult to perceive. We know, as we review our personal histories, that all the disparate events of our existence are somehow connected. It seems at times as though some of our actions and thoughts were hardly ours. We might wonder why we ever thought as we did, or how we managed to survive, or what made us behave in such a manner, or who gave us the resources to accomplish our tasks.

Yet we know that all these experiences belong to us. They are interwoven into the tapestry of our lives even though the patterns are not always intended and take shape at times almost of their own will. We recognize the texture of the tapestry as our handiwork because there are threads of continuity and connection.

This continuity seems to be woven by a "spirit" in each person which enables the individual moments to become united as a whole or entirety. These apparently disconnected moments belong to the completeness or integrity of a person even though there seems to be something arbitrary about some of them. At times, we shrug our shoulders at the incomprehensibility of

it all, but we recognize, nonetheless, that this was our life and the way our world went.

When we consider the Church itself, we find the same process operative. Here too, a "Spirit," the Spirit of God, we believe, holds the history of the Church together as an entirety and enables it to act in accord with its own nature. The way the Church develops is not always predictable beforehand nor clear in retrospect.

The Church, like each of us, acts at times against its own best interests or resists its own Spirit. There are dark and sinful moments in the Church's history, and so the Church must be rescued and redeemed, reformed and renewed by the very Spirit it has hindered.

In the Church, the Spirit links the past with the present and makes the future continuous with all that went before it.

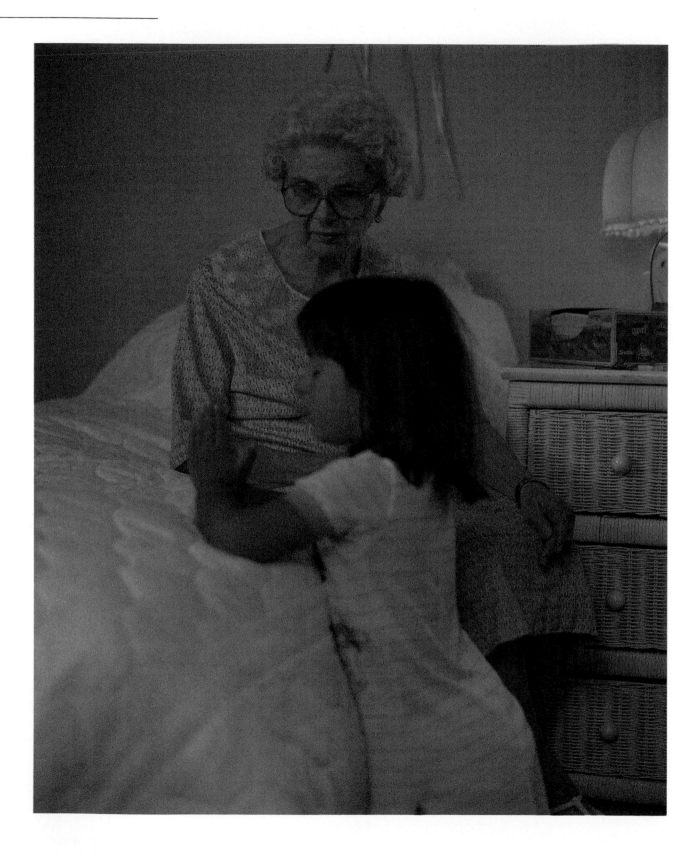

The Church will go on as long as its negative experiences and mistakes do not so distort the integrity of the Church that it ceases to be what it was meant to be. Catholics believe that this can never happen to the Church, that the Church is somehow infallibly guided so that its errors never become fatal nor its sins terminal. Catholics believe that God's Spirit saves the Church from its excesses, just as that same Spirit makes the Church a marvel and a miracle to behold. On the eve of its third millennium of history, Catholics look back and are astonished at the longevity of the Church and at the goodness it has brought into the world. It has never lost Christ nor ceased to remember him. It has never failed to preach the Gospel. It has struggled time and time again to give

love as its Master once gave love to it.

The process by which this continuity occurs might be called ''tradition.'' The word ''tradition'' has a Latin root; it means to hand something on to someone else.

Each of our lives has a ''tradition.'' That ''tradition'' is the mysterious way we hand on our life to others. A parent gives his or her life spirit to children; a teacher does this with pupils, or a preacher with a congregation. People often perceive the ''spirit'' of the person and gain life from it even though they do not agree with all the words or deeds of the person who influences them. People have a capacity to interpret the words or deeds of another in accord with the ''spirit'' of the person. We observe that a certain person did not really

(photo left) Each of our lives has a "tradition." That "tradition" is the mysterious way we hand on our life to others.

ALTERNATIVE COMMUNITIES

The items we listed as part of the Catholic Tradition are brought to our attention constantly. In the course of each year, Catholics make contact with teaching about Mary or Peter, about sacraments and conciliar decisions.

In addition to these encounters with Tradition, the Church develops its Tradition in another way by fostering creative community life. Formal religious life, with vows and structure, with clear references to celibacy and poverty, is a post-biblical phenomenon.

The witness of learning and love, of healing and social justice, of contemplation and compassion given by religious communities has been impressive. No other Christian Church has made so much of these communities. In the Catholic Church, the holiness of marriage is paralleled by the holiness of these celibate fraternities and sisterhoods. It is noteworthy that the Catholic

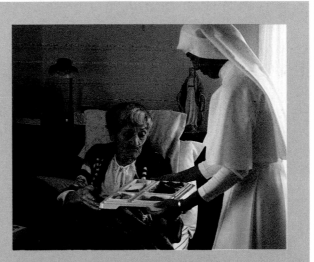

Church has emphasized in its Tradition the sacramentality of marriage and the value of celibate community life. Both sacramental marriage and formal religious communities are states of life endowed with canonical recognition and public vows. Both of these Christian choices enrich the Tradition and life of the Church.

36

mean what he or she said or that a particular action ought to be evaluated in this manner rather than in another way.

All of this happens to the Church as well and is at issue in our acceptance of the Church.

The "tradition" of the Church is its act of handing on its life to successive generations of Christians. The Church gives over to the future not only its memory of Christ and the Eucharist, not only its faith in Easter and its Scripture but indeed its very life and Spirit. This Spirit links the past with the present and makes the future continuous with all that went before it.

A Guiding Tradition

We have yet to consider a question we have been working toward and left unanswered so far. This question concerns how we might discern the key decisions or moments in the Church's tradition, moments which are neither marginal, trivial nor reversible, moments which are not negative, counterproductive or out of character moments which are indeed of lasting significance and help define the Church as what it is.

We need to ask ourselves whether all the reality of the Church, all its important and pivotal experiences are reflected in Scripture or whether another resource is available to the Church for the continuity of its life. Indeed, we might wonder whether the Church can even read its own Scripture properly if it does not have a Spirit or Tradition which enables it to place that Scripture properly in its life and to give adequate weight and meaning to the words of Scripture, words which are sometimes

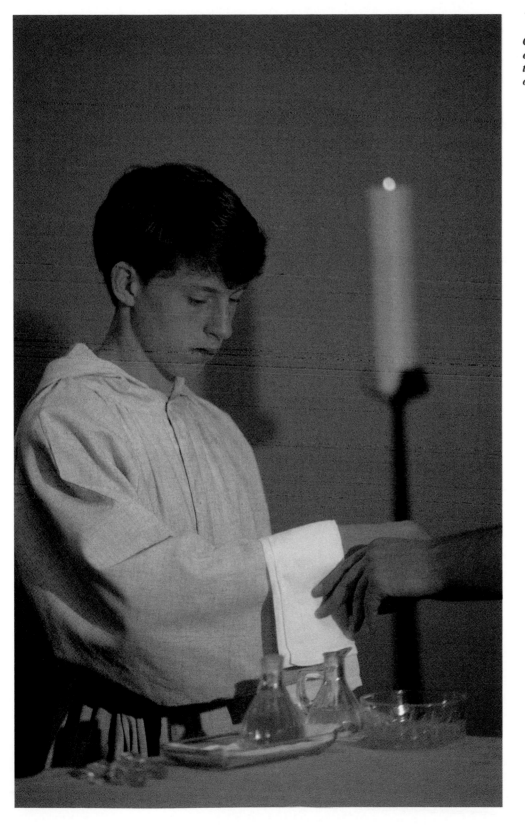

Grace is God's loving energy at work within the Church and within our souls.

ambiguous and even harsh unless seen in the proper light.

We might cite a few of the pivotal decisions or affirmations the Catholic Church has made. These are not clearly present in Scripture, if at all, and yet have become a vital part of the Church's life over the course of its history.

One of the first of these is the role of Mary, the Mother of Jesus, in the theology and spirituality of the Church. Mary seems to have a lesser role to play in the New Testament than she does in the subsequent history of the Church. The Church has struggled for centuries to clarify Mary's position and to locate it in the proper context. She is, in Catholic theology, thoroughly human and yet sinless; a creature like us and yet the Mother of God; someone who dies as we do and yet is assumed into heaven.

Another item concerns the sacramental system. Over the centuries the Catholic Church formally defined marriage as a sacrament even though other Christian Churches do not and even though the New Testament gives us few, if any, indications that it ought to be. It has had to work, furthermore, with the proper way to evaluate ordination, to link it with lay life and yet to make it distinct.

Even the place of sacraments such as Baptism and Eucharist which the other Christian Churches recognize as important ritual actions, even these need to be clarified and assigned an identity. Catholics, for example, celebrate Eucharist with a frequency and ritual intensity which only the Eastern Orthodox Churches approximate. In Catholic consciousness, the Eucharist is a permanent sign of belonging to the Church and accep-

PENTECOST/THE SPIRIT IN THE CHURCH

The liturgical feast of Pentecost is often called the "birthday" of the Church. It is called this because, until Pentecost, the disciples and apostles perform no public work in the name of Jesus. There is no preaching until Pentecost. Before Pentecost, the followers of Jesus mourn for him, in private, and are beset with fear and confusion. Even those who knew Jesus intimately and who encountered the risen Christ could be immobilized by doubt and insecurity.

At the Baptism of Jesus, the heavens were torn open and the light of God illumined the mind and heart of Jesus for mission. Jesus begins to preach only after this event. In Pentecost, the disciples sense the opening of the heavens as the fire of God's Spirit enlightens and emboldens them for

ministry. They begin to preach after Pentecost.

The Spirit is Christ's gift to the Church. It comes with Christ's promise that the Spirit will never abandon the Church. It is the Spirit which enables the Church again and again to find Christ in new ways.

tance by it.

A further point is the place of Peter in the Church and whether Peter is to have successors. The Catholic Church accords Peter a more prominent role in its interpretation of the New Testament than that given him by the other Christian churches. It develops from this understanding of Peter's role the distinctive feature of the papacy and identifies the papacy as having a unique mission in preserving the unity of the Church.

A final item we might cite is the importance of Ecumenical Councils in the Church's history. These impressive assemblies of cardinals and bishops, of theologians and laity, of monks and priests, of princes and prelates have, over the centuries, made perhaps the most crucial decisions for the Church. The collegial and collaborative character of these meetings serves to balance the papal office with a more consultative and deliberative voice for the Church at large.

The list could be extended but it need not be. It is sufficient to note that the Spirit moves through the Church and makes it something other than a community which remembers Jesus. The Church is also a gathering of believers who contribute century by century to the life of Jesus as Church and to the very completion of Christ in history. Jesus is not only risen in his Easter body but is also alive in the body of the Church. This is the source of the Church's Tradition. Jesus, as he promised, did not leave us alone but is with us for all time, as an active and living Presence.

The Church is a gathering of believers who contribute century by century to the life of Jesus as Church and to the very completion of Christ in history.

4

WORD AND SCRIPTURE

We have made reference throughout these chapters to Scripture. No Christian community is formed without recourse to Scripture as a guide and basis for its faith.

Scripture is, perhaps, the most concrete of the basic factors contributing to the origins of the Church and the one which gives us the clearest indications of what a Christian community should be. The Christ we considered in the first chapter is not present to us physically and historically. The Liturgy we celebrate is not available in the form the early

"He comes to us as One unknown, without a name; as of old by the lakeside he came to those who knew him not. He speaks to us the same word: 'Follow thou me!'" (Albert Schweitzer).

Scripture explores the successes and failures, the ideas and emotions, the problems and solutions which the Church struggled with as it sought to become a believing community in a structured manner. It gives us, therefore, access to the beginning with a directness and immediacy that the other experiences we surveyed do not. For this, as well as other reasons, Scripture has been a source of life for the Christian community in an altogether unique manner over the centuries.

For all its accessibility, however, Scripture is not easy to interpret. The written word can illuminate and mystify at one and the same time. Americans are aware, for example, of how difficult the United States Constitution is to understand and apply. That document is only two centuries old, and it is written in a language that the scholars and legislators who interpret it still use. Even with abundant records of the debates and intentions of the framers of the Constitution, the nation is not always convinced it knows what the words actually intend.

Memory

Scripture is studied across a chasm of time, by people throughout the world whose language and culture differ enormously from those who wrote the text we have. For this reason, Scripture has both united and divided the Christian community over the centuries. Nonetheless, it remains an impressive resource, and it gives all Christians a vocabulary and a tangible standard for their lives and for their Church structures.

Scripture is a magnificent summary

Christians followed. It is difficult to deduce from it distinct ideas about how the Church should function. Tradition is the most elusive of all these original elements.

Scripture, however, exists in the very words the early Christian community employed. It is composed in the thought patterns of those first believers, by those who actually witnessed Christ and were present at the Last Supper, the crucifixion and the first Easter morning.

of all the original elements we have considered in these opening chapters. It is last in the line, chronologically speaking, of the constitutive factors which make up the identity of the Church. It comes after Christ, after the Breaking of the Bread, after the force of Tradition. And yet it draws these together in a remarkable manner. The experience of Christ conveyed in Scripture is reflected through the liturgical worship of the first few decades after the departure of Christ and through the formative influence of Tradition which had already shaped the community in some way. By the time the early community put its faith into writing, the memory of Jesus was no longer a mere historical recollection of him but an emotional remembrance charged with hope and love. The disciples wished to give us a history of Jesus by witnessing to their devotion. Scripture becomes the record of all that Jesus meant to them and of all that had happened to them not only while he was with them but also after he had departed. Scripture proclaims the power of Christ but also the openness of the community to the influence of Jesus and of his Spirit.

There is a false assumption in our society that the memory of someone is most precise, objective and closer to the ''truth'' if it is reported by an observer who has no vested interest in that memory and who relays it to us with the detachment of a camera or a computer. We might ask ourselves whether this assumption is a good one.

If we had, for example, a complete videotape of all the actions and words of Jesus, would we be able to interpret them better? We have, do we not, full accessibility to presidents and prominent people in our day and yet we do

not agree on what they are about, what they mean, what their motives are, what to make of them. No matter how much data the human mind receives, it is not relieved of its responsibility to judge and to evaluate, to interpret and to decide. Each person must conclude that another is good or bad, believable or not, trustworthy or unreliable.

It is unfortunate that our society assumes that people who have no love or care for another are those who can give us a more accurate analysis of

Who we are is always located in who the others were who entered our lives and whom we now remember.

that person. We grant, of course, that those who favor another may not always see the whole picture, especially in its negative and distorted aspects. The idea, however, that anyone of us approaches data with no personal assumptions is patently unconvincing.

We sense that we ourselves and those we love are best interpreted by those to whom we have revealed ourselves most intimately. We reveal less when we are in the company of those who are indifferent and hostile. It is, of course, true that those close to us do not always see us in our professional and public life, yet the assessment they offer is in most cases as near the truth of our identity as we are likely to get.

Scripture, therefore, clarifies Christ and presents him as a mystery at one and the same time. It gives us a portrait of who he was by those who knew him best and loved him fully. Such a portrait can never be provided again. The portrait is, admittedly, an amalgam of data and belief, of reason and emotion, of memory and passion.

In our own lives, when we remember someone, we remember not only that person but also ourselves in relationship to that person. A camera or a computer does not do this. These instruments and machines are not, of course, human.

Human memory of another is always a memory of the self. This is what makes it so appealing and valuable. Who we are is always located in who the others were who entered our lives and whom we now remember.

When the early Christian community wrote about Christ, it wrote about itself as well. Scripture, therefore,

links us with those early Christians in affection and faith rather than by data and knowledge. It gives us enough to satisfy our love even if there is not enough to satisfy our intellects.

If we are to have a portrait of Jesus, we who believe in him and love him, we need to ask ourselves whether we would rather have this drawn for us by scholars and research people or by those who loved Christ. This question touches on the very nature of the Christian community. Is the Christian community primarily about knowledge or is it about love?

We must not, in this discussion, become simplistic. In a sense, the Christian community is about both knowledge and love. A human response to a person must not be so naive or thoughtless that one ceases to be responsible. A great deal of harm has been done in Christian history by charlatans and even by well-intentioned people who appealed so completely to love as the only norm that they invited the abandonment of all reason. Quite obviously, we are not suggesting this.

(photo left) "If we think of the dead in the biblical image as 'a cloud of witnesses,' they are not just spectators from a distance of one, ten, fifty, or four hundred years; they are contemporaries cheering us on" (David H. C. Read).

(photo below) "Gratitude is the heart's memory" (French proverb).

It is love, nonetheless, which has priority. This love, when it is genuine, impels us to have as much knowledge as possible about the person we love. Love is always enriched by the truth, not diminished by it.

The infallibility and inspiration of Scripture may be present less in the objective validity of its data than in its capacity to give us a Christ whom the Christian community has loved intensely through the centuries. If the point of Scripture was to help us believe and be devoted to Christ, it has succeeded remarkably. If its point was to make Christ real to us, it is an eminently realistic document.

Worship

Scripture is not only a written life story of Jesus. It is also a liturgical document. Scripture was fashioned by a community which understood Jesus, after he departed, in the Breaking of the Bread. All the power of the cross and the empty tomb entered into their liturgical assemblies and helped them to see new dimensions and depths in such a life. The passage of time and the experience of worship clarified Jesus for the early Christians. This clarity was not only intellectual. It was also emotional and devotional. Jesus was not only proclaimed as Son of God but loved as Son of God.

We know, from our own experience, that the life of those we love is not over in their dying. Death and absence enter into the process of our understanding who they were when they were here.

The Christian community perceived that the death and absence of Jesus were overcome not only in the Easter event but also in the Breaking of the

PAST AND FUTURE

The Christian community has always tried to keep a balance between past and future. It looks back as it looks forward. Its Christmas memories of Jesus are also hopes for his final return. Its Easter memories seek the Second Coming of the Risen and Glorified Christ.

The Liturgy of the Christian community is a tension between the cross on which Jesus died and the cry of Maranatha, "Come, Lord Jesus," which is a herald of the future. Bread is broken not only in fidelity to all that was but in anticipation of all that is yet to be. It is not only present time at our assemblies of the Christian community, not only past time in our recollections of Jesus, but Advent time as we wait for the birth of Christ to occur in a wholly new way.

The Scripture, which is a record of the past, is also a Tradition telling us that the meaning of the past is in the future and that the future is present in our midst as Scripture is proclaimed and bread and wine become nourishment and hope for a pilgrim people.

47

"Injustice anywhere is a threat to justice everywhere" (Martin Luther King, Jr.).

Bread. The Eucharist was a celebration of Christ's Presence. It was not a memorial service for a departed but finally deceased person. It was an act of faith in the Christ who was alive and active in the midst of those who broke bread in his memory.

Jesus gave the early disciples no instructions or even a suggestion that they write about him. Had he done so, they would have told us this as they wrote. The writing came out of the breaking of the bread and out of the community's Easter faith. Easter and the Eucharist led to the foundation of the Church and the creation of Scripture.

Through the centuries, the early Christian community understood this. This is why the Church gives the reading of Scripture prominence in its worship and liturgical services. The Scripture's privileged moment is the Liturgy. Scripture seldom registers with us more strongly than when it is read at worship.

If we believe that Christ is present in a special way in our assemblies, then the reading about that very same Christ, at that moment, is impressive. In this manner, the last of the original elements in the creation of the Church, namely Scripture, is linked with the first item we cited, namely Christ. There is coherence and consistency among the differing experiences that form the Church from the beginning.

Scripture captures Tradition and falls short of it. It gives us all the main lines that Tradition will pursue through the centuries. But it also leaves unfinished and unsaid many of the developments which Christ promised that the Spirit would come to teach us.

Just as Scripture does not so exhaust the reality of Christ that Liturgy has nothing to offer, so Scripture does not so complete Christ that Tradition has nothing to teach. The interplay of these various elements helps to keep the community creative and rescues its faith from being a faith merely about the past. Everything is given and nothing is finished.

Each Christian community brings to Liturgy and Tradition nuances which contribute to the full reality and

The writing of Scripture came out of the early Christian community's experience of Eucharist and out of their Easter faith.

identity of Christ. Thus, each Christian community is linked with the early Church not only in affection and faith for Christ, not only in the Presence of Christ as we break bread together but in the making of the Christian Tradition by the power of the Spirit.

The original experience of the early Church in memory, Liturgy, Scripture and apostolic Tradition serves as a guide and message for all the centuries which follow. No later era or subsequent community of Christians will serve as a norm in the same way or as decisively. But a norm is not a totality. Other things need to be said and done, and these are neither repetitions of the past nor mere applications of it. These later developments continue to constitute and complete who Christ is, a Christ so overwhelming and massive in his meaning that no one generation of Christians, not even the first, can express him fully.

By the end of the first century, all these powerful forces were in place. They would impel the Christian community through the centuries as surely as the original explosion at the beginning of creation would impel matter through the universe of time and space.

One day, in the Second Coming, the original forces which launched the community, its memories and liturgies, its Tradition and Scripture, will encounter the visible Christ once more, when history shall have run its course. Future believers will know this Christ as who he is because the People of God will have dealt with him through all the millennia along the lines it first knew him in the beginning. He will one day come among his own and his own will receive him.

The memory of the Christian community will then become encounter: the Breaking of the Bread will yield to the embrace of Christ; Tradition will culminate in Presence; and all of Scripture will become a hymn of praise from a community which kept faith and was not disappointed, a community which held onto love and was not finally disillusioned.

"Two are better than one....If the one falls, the other will lift up his companion....Where a lone person may be overcome, two together can resist" (cf. Ecclesiastes 4:9-12).

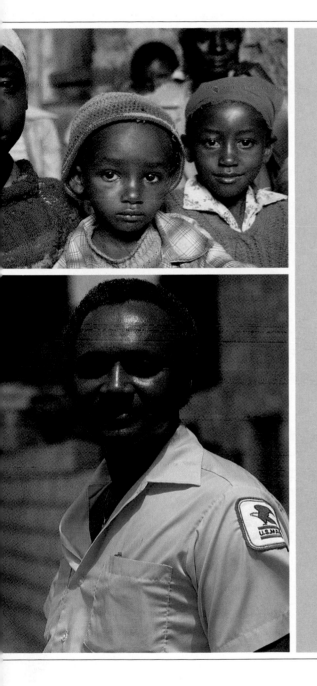

"By divine institution the holy Church is ordered and governed with a wonderful diversity. 'For just as in one body we have many members, yet all the members have not the same functions, so we the many, are one body in Christ, but severally members of one another' (*Romans* 12:4-5).A

"There is, therefore, one chosen People of God: 'one Lord, one faith, one baptism' (*Ephesians* 4:5); there is a common dignity of members deriving from their rebirth in Christ, a common grace as children, a common vocation to perfection, one salvation, one hope and undivided charity. In Christ and in the Church there is, then, no inequality arising from race or nationality, social condition or sex, for 'there is neither Jew nor Greek; there is neither slave nor free person; there is neither male nor female. For you are all one in Christ Jesus' " (*Galatians* 3:28; cf. *Colossians* 3:11).

adapted from
Vatican Council II 1964
DOGMATIC CONSTITUTION ON THE CHURCH *IV:32*

II. Visions:
Hope and Commitment

5

SYMBOLS AND SACRAMENTS

No living organism can stay as it is and still maintain life. Change is the essence of life. It is also a central force in development and maturity.

The Church is no exception. It needs to grow and adapt, to develop and adjust, or else it will lose its life.

Change, however, is an ambiguous experience. On the one hand, it is exhilarating. When one beholds a child learning to speak or beginning to walk, the joy on the child's face is a clear sign of satisfaction and

(photo below, right)
"But when the kindness and generous love of God our savior appeared...he saved us through the bath of rebirth and renewal by the Holy Spirit...."
(cf. Titus 3:4-5).

exuberance. On the other hand, there is frustration and fear in change. Words do not always come readily and people begin to expect more of the child. Walking is not easily maneuvered; falls are frequent and painful. Life itself urges the child to go on even though the child may be tempted to retreat into silence or immobility.

Something of this same experience is present in the history of the Church. There is, however, an important difference. One cannot say that the Church grows beyond its origins so that the later Church is more mature than the early Church was. The Church begins so splendidly that it looks back to the beginning as a norm for all its future life.

This is different from the situation which occurs with each of us. We do not look back to our first years of life in order to guide us in all our subsequent actions.

The Church, however, begins with Jesus Christ and Easter, with the Last Supper and the faithful repetition of this in the early communities, with the gift of the Spirit in its fullness, and with the Scripture written under the guidance of those who knew and loved Christ. How could the later Church be more than this? How can one say that the Church can still grow and develop after so much has been accomplished at the very beginning?

There have been Christians through the centuries who maintained that the Church must be literally and precisely that which it once was. All subsequent Christian history is seen as a deviation unless it repeats the original pattern. The Church, in effect, becomes a museum, keeping intact something which must never change.

In such a conception of the Church, the elements we considered in the first four chapters are woodenly and rigidly evaluated. Christ's words are interpreted literally and with no reference to their temporal and social context. Liturgy is conducted as it might have been in the first century. All adaptations are seen as corruptions of the standard. The role of the Spirit and Tradition in the life of the Church is limited to what happened to the first generation of Christians. Later history is judged superfluous and even dangerous. Proponents of these ideas cite eloquently the sins of contemporary Christians. They fail to see that the early Church had sins in it also and that some of the decisions made by the New Testament Church were not always the best.

The decision to hold all things in common, for example, did not work.

The serving of elaborate dinners as a way of celebrating the Last Supper became burdensome and divisive and the relegation of women to lesser roles in some Christian communities was not praiseworthy. The emphasis on charismatic structures for the Church in other Christian communities became chaotic and confusing.

A Living Community

The Christian community at large, in all its diverse Churches, has not gone this route of limiting change to an absolute minimum. The early Christians themselves did not consider their experience of church so rigid a norm that no subsequent development could occur. The New Testament is filled with change as adaptations are needed. It is the clarity of the memory and the Presence of Jesus in the early Church which is impressive, not necessarily its capacity to apply the message of Jesus to all the changing circumstances of first-century life.

The Church through the centuries grows and matures as it makes Christ present and active in different ways, in different areas of life, in different parts of the world, with new languages and cultural idioms. In this sense, it makes more of Christ than he was in his historical life.

We ourselves mature as we apply our experience to new life situations. The Church grows in this manner as well. It deepens its sense of Christ as it sees Christ in new experiences and moments.

We began this chapter by alluding to the change which happens as a child begins to talk and to walk. The Church through the centuries learns to talk in varied ways, to increase its vocabulary

beyond that of Hebrew, Greek and Latin, to define Christ for the world and for all time, to interpret the words of Christ with meanings not originally intended, perhaps, but authentically possible.

The Church through the centuries learns to walk in new ways, to experience the limits of its power and the strength that vulnerability sometimes gives it, to become confident in adapting the message of Jesus to political, moral and economic issues not envisioned by the early Church, to

The Church through the centuries learns to walk in new ways...to become confident in adapting the message of Jesus to political, moral and economic issues not envisioned by the early Church.

"Special words are used to describe such an event as Baptism: a rebirth, an enlightenment, a new creation, a new life, people becoming the temple of the Holy Spirit....and at the very heart of Baptism: the presence of God to an individual" (Kenan Osborne).

perceive that Jesus' message has a resiliency and stability, a universality and concreteness that the early Church could hardly imagine.

This change becomes the glory of the Church and forces it to deal with Christ profoundly, as challenge after challenge is presented, and as solutions are found within the context of the Church's original beginnings and intention. The change, ironically, leads the Church to appreciate its origins more, to preserve them better and to see them even more clearly as a norm.

Change does not take the Church beyond Christ but more deeply into him. The steps away from the original intentions and words of Jesus become the means by which the Church comes to complete Christ by extending his message and love through all peoples and all times.

One of the most effective changes the Church makes is the development of its symbolic or sacramental system.

Jesus himself initiates the process by urging the disciples to baptize and to break bread in his memory. When

Jesus is present physically to the community, these ritual actions are less important. When Jesus has gone, they become powerful means of expressing faith in his continuing presence.

We know in our own life experience that the physical distance or absence of those we love leads us to use more symbols with them. When we are away, we might send flowers or gifts; we might write letters or carry photographs or souvenirs to remind us of the other person. If death occurs, we turn almost completely to symbols. We light candles and preserve keepsakes, hand down heirlooms and repeat rituals we have done with that person. The symbols become impressive because the absence of the person and the consequent abiding memory cannot be grasped in words. Absence, paradoxically, becomes a way to presence.

When Jesus is gone, the Christian community symbolizes his enduring Presence and their faith in it. They turn to bread and wine, to oil and candles, to music and writing, and they make these crucial to their worship and memory, their Tradition and Scripture. The movement into symbols is a long process of growth and maturity, envisioning new methods for keeping contact with a Jesus who is both absent and present to the community.

Sacraments of Initiation

In all the ritual actions and vital symbols the community celebrates, Baptism has a special role. One might observe that Baptism and Eucharist will become pivotal sacraments in the Catholic system. Indeed, they will also

be affirmed by the different Christian Churches through the centuries as important sacred signs, even when the other sacraments in the Catholic Tradition are not taken over by these Churches into their worship.

Baptism is a sacrament of initiation into the Catholic community and,

"There is in us more kinship with the divine than we are able to believe. The souls of all are candles of the Lord, lit on the cosmic way..." (Abraham Heschel).

"Save your people, and bless your inheritance; feed them and carry them forever" (Psalms 28:9)!

indeed, into the entire Christian assembly of Churches. Once one is baptized, other Christian Churches respect and honor this. The Baptism is not repeated if one goes to another Christian Church. There is something so fundamentally Christian about this commitment by the candidate for Baptism and by the Church which receives the commitment that it becomes valid for life for the baptized and for the Christian Churches.

Baptism is a sign of commitment to the Person and program of Jesus Christ. The water and the trinitarian formula symbolize the consecration at the beginning of Christ's ministry, when the Father speaks as the Son is baptized in the River Jordan with the bestowal of the Spirit. Baptism is, therefore, a ministerial commissioning, a priestly sacrament, one which gives a believer standing in the community and readies that person for whatever ministry God's call of the person and the needs of the community require.

Baptism, for the purpose of this book on the Church especially, can be seen as an ecclesial sacrament which creates a formal, visible and intentionally permanent relationship with the Church. There is a clear sign in the ritual of this sacrament that the candidate is committed to a personal relationship with Christ. And, yet, this sacrament incorporates the person into a community and its tradition. The person is baptized by a designated minister of the Church, in a ceremony the Church recognizes as its own, for service in the Church and witness to its beliefs and moral life, its disciplines and customs. One is said to be not only baptized but baptized Catholic or Anglican or Orthodox or Lutheran.

The Catholic community believes that another sacrament, Confirmation, completes Baptism. This does not imply that Baptism is not integral on its own but that a special consecration in oil signifies other dimensions of this initiation. If Baptism symbolizes the beginning of the Church's ministry to the world in the River Jordan, Confirmation represents the beginning of the Church's ministry to the world in Pentecost. It is the Spirit and the special gifts of Christian life which are emphasized in this sacrament. Confirmation re-enforces the notion of the Church as a spiritual and charismatic community. Baptism stresses commitment to the Person of Christ; Confirmation accentuates the gift of the Spirit to the person confirmed. Baptism orients a believer to Church membership and ministry; Confirmation disposes that same person to prophecy and proclamation. The fact that the Church is founded on an apostolic structure is more clearly

"Christ left to his followers a pledge of hope and food for the journey in the sacrament of faith...as a supper of fellowship and a foretaste of the heavenly banquet" (cf. Vatican II: Church in Modern World, #38).

"God of mercy, through this holy anointing give Joseph comfort in his suffering. When he is afraid, give him courage,... when dejected, afford him hope, and when alone, assure him of the support of your holy people" (from the Rite of Anointing).

manifest in Baptism; its foundation on prophets as well is more obvious in Confirmation.

The third sacrament of initiation is Eucharist. We have dealt with this in the second chapter. We mention it now so that we can see that the progression from Baptism through Confirmation reaches its fulfillment in Eucharist. The candidate who is now cleansed and made priestly, now consecrated and gifted, is given the Body and Blood of Christ and brought to the table of the Lord as a full member of the family. Communion with Christ is complete, and this is signified by our intense identification with Christ which the Eucharist achieves. In Baptism, we are made the People of God; in Confirmation, the community of the Spirit; in Eucharist, the Body of Christ.

Anointing and Reconciliation

The sacramental system is one of the Catholic Church's most distinctive signs. No other Christian Church has a more elaborate and comprehensive

sacramental life. In no other Christian Church, for example, are Anointing, Reconciliation and Eucharist celebrated more frequently. No other Christian Church has developed its theology of Marriage and Orders, of Baptism and Confirmation more fully.

For Catholics, it is participation in the sacramental life of the Church which gives the most profound sense of belonging to the community. Access to the Church's worship service of Scripture and preaching is not a fully satisfying experience for a Catholic if that person is excluded from Communion.

The Catholic community is characterized by its optimism and by its belief in the essential goodness of humanity. And, yet, it has at the very core of its life two sacraments which focus on evil and failure.

In the life of a Christian, Anointing is reserved for the emergence of pain and disability, and at times for the imminence of death. Reconciliation requires the consciousness and recognition of sin for its celebration. These two sacraments may, ironically, account for the optimism in the

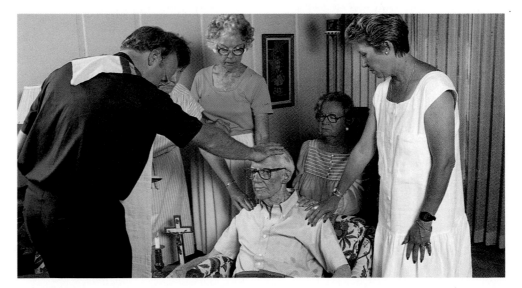

The Church defines itself as a community of love.

Catholic Church concerning the human condition. Death and sin are anticipated and expected by the sacramental system, and yet there is a conviction that these are passing and not permanent features of Christian life.

The sacraments of initiation have an enduring quality about them. Baptism and Confirmation are never repeated. Eucharist is envisioned as a regular and constant experience. But Anointing and Reconciliation are occasional sacraments; they celebrate something which is passing in a believer's life rather than something which will remain. Even death is seen as a process in which life is changed rather than taken away.

The Catholic Church expects us to sin but does not take it for granted. It asks us to be conscious of our sins, to recognize them and resolve to be done

with them, even as it tells us our sins are now of no account and we are to celebrate only our innocence.

The sacraments are not only external actions of the Church. They also reveal its inner life. And so, as we participate in the sacramental system we also learn something about the nature of the Church. We are made aware of its sense of mission and ministry, of gift and Spirit, of its conviction that Christ is still with us in bread and wine, of its total trust in God to take away our death and to abolish all our sins.

Holy Orders and Matrimony

The Church defines itself as a community of love. In the sacraments of Orders and Marriage, it celebrates love and the way that love comes into

The Church has raised the personal bonding and sexual love of marriage to the highest order by bringing it into its sacramental system.

the community's life.

Leadership in the Christian community is a subtle blend of the person's conviction of a call from God, of the community's affirmation of that call and of the universal Church's conferral of Orders. This conferral signifies that the ordained minister has responsibilities to the Church at large and to the Church of all ages.

Christ and the Spirit are invoked in the ritual of Orders so that all may know that ordination is not a person's right or a local community's exclusive prerogative but, in some way, an action of the whole Church. The ordained minister is accountable to Christ and to the Gospel, to the Liturgy and the Tradition of the Church, in a word, to all the original elements in the Church. The minister is also answerable to the community the minister serves and to the Church at large.

The ordained minister symbolizes Christ in an indelible and unique manner and becomes a focal point for the unity of a small community of Christians. Leadership is so influential

in the conduct of a community's life that the Church gives this office careful scrutiny and the solemn affirmation of its sacramental system. The ordained minister is referred to as someone who must pastor God's People, giving life and love for the community's sake.

The Second Vatican Council gave, perhaps, the most beautiful definition of marriage in all Catholic history. It called it "an intimate partnership of marital life and love" (**The Church in the Modern World**, #48).

The Church has raised the personal bonding and sexual love of marriage to the highest order by bringing it into its sacramental system. Marriage, for a Catholic, is not only contract and covenant, not only vows and commitment, but a sacrament. This means that it is a sign of Christ's Presence and grace on the most intensive level the Church can signify.

Marriage is not only for the couple and for Christ but also for the Church. And, so, the Church frequently celebrates this sacrament during the Liturgy of the Eucharist. It involves most of the sacramental system in this celebration. The couple is expected to be baptized and confirmed and to promise this for their children. The Church requests that the couple be fully reconciled to the Church. In the normal course of events, an ordained minister, the pastoral leader of the community, is expected to witness and preside at the wedding.

Marriage is, perhaps, the most universal and joyful of all human experiences. It is celebrated with elaborate ceremony throughout the world by all cultures and peoples. The Church brings the life and words of Christ into this event. And it declares, thereby, that family is at the center of the Church's very nature and, indeed, that the family gives the Church a powerful model for the way the life of the Church is to be lived.

Calling and Encounter

The elements in the original founding of the Church were simple and direct. In the course of time, the Church derives from its memory of Christ its memories of his Baptism and gift of the Spirit, of his Last Supper and words of pardon, of his healing and summoning of disciples for special service, of his celebration of the love of men and women in marriage. The Church creates sacramental signs which come from the light of its Tradition and from its reflection on Scripture. All this culminates in a remarkable way in the assembly of the community for the Breaking of Bread.

The sacraments move in three directions. They recall Christ's life, preeminently, as we have seen. They are, secondly, finely attuned to the life stages in the development of a person:

birth (Baptism) and maturity (Confirmation), family meals (Eucharist) and forgiveness (Reconciliation), sickness and sorrow (Anointing), service (Ordination) and love (Marriage).

In a special way, the sacraments move in the direction of the Church's own life. The sacraments become the convergence point of Christian discipleship, personal meaning and Church participation.

The Church learns from its celebration of sacraments how bound it is to Christ and to each individual person. It gives sacraments to people one by one. The Church teaches the individual that membership in the Church is neither a transient nor superficial commitment but a sacred calling and an encounter with Christ.

The ordained minister must pastor God's People, giving life and love for the community's sake.

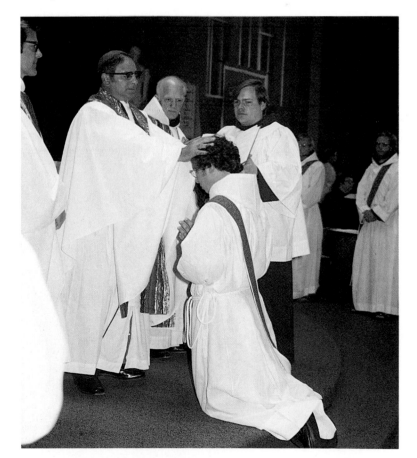

6

AUTHORITY AND CONSCIENCE

The question of authority and conscience
is one of the most delicate in any church
system. Indeed, it is an aspect of life which is
seldom fully settled in any institution or
family. Even when the model invoked is a
clear and unambiguous one, namely the
military model, there is still room for conscience and dissent.

A soldier is expected to disobey orders,
even in time of war, if asked to violate higher
norms of action. Thus, a soldier ordered to
massacre innocent civilians and children

"Let all things be done decently and in order" (cf. 1 Corinthians 14:40).

would be held accountable to military justice and punished for **obeying** the order.

Nazi officers who participated in the Holocaust were dealt with severely by an international tribunal after World War II. They were convicted of crimes against humanity even though they maintained that they were only obeying orders. The tribunal brought them to justice because the Nazi system itself did not do this and because they were expected to have consciences which should have kept them from obeying such horrible and grisly orders.

A pilot asked to bomb a civilian target would be obliged, in the terms of Catholic morality, to refuse to comply even if it meant the end of his career. In this case, the pilot would be punished by the military for **disobeying** orders.

If even the military, in time of war, must build into its system of authority some measure of resiliency and a role for conscience, then surely the relationship between authority and conscience is not an easy one. The military model, in time of war, is perhaps the most persuasive example for the exercise of authority over and against all claims of individual dissent. Yet, in this instance, all is not clear. Even in this case it will not do merely to say that obedience is always expected or that authority is always right.

On the other hand, the right of all people to do exactly as they please would lead to chaos. Every human society has laws so that people are restrained from erratic, capricious and destructive behavior.

Even if people claim they are acting in accord with their conscience, societies will restrain them from irresponsible actions and require that their consciences or, at the very least, their activities be properly directed.

Homicide is not justifiable because the murderer reasons it is in accord with conscience. Sexual abuse is a crime even if the assailant claims the personal right to do this. Bigamy is prohibited even if one's religious system gives this option.

The closer one comes in an institutional structure to a family model rather than to a military model, the more difficult it becomes to formulate a solution to this vexing question of conscience and authority. Families, of their nature, allow large areas of latitude, necessitated, in part, by the priority of personal values and love in a family and, in part, by the fact that they prepare their members for eventual autonomy. To the extent that families engender only life-long docility, they fail.

The model for the Church is closer to the family and community model than it is to the military or corporate model. In a sense, this makes the authority-conscience conflict more intense.

The Church as an institution cannot function fully within the family model nor with the facility a family has for creative interaction. Church members do not have the immediate, intimate, direct relationship a family does. Nor do its members by and large have the investment of life in the Church as institution that people do in their families. Even here, however, all is not clear. Families, after all, do break up and fail.

If the military model is too authoritarian for the Church and the family model is too informal, what model ought the Church to use?

As in everything else, the Church must refer to its original basic elements: the memory of Jesus, the Breaking of the Bread, Tradition and Scripture.

Authority and Love

Jesus Christ did teach with authority. Although he is frequently opposed to rigid structures, unbending laws, and autocratic rulers, he also makes clear that God demands things from us. The Beatitudes list a series of expectations; the norms for judgment at the end of time ("I was hungry and you fed me...") enumerate a set of obligations. The Law is not to be abolished but fulfilled. Prophets are to be tested; true disciples are to be recognized. The Twelve are clearly designated, and they are given careful instructions as they set out on mission.

Taxes are to be paid; the Jewish practice of divorce is rejected; authority is given to the leaders of the community.

Jesus himself and the community's memory of him oblige the Church, therefore, to exercise authority in his name, for the sake of his people and his message.

Jesus, however, does not make the issue easy. He himself breaks laws and rules. He envisions a world in which the first are last. The model for authority is the little child he holds in his arms or the shepherd who leaves all

"The family is a place where different generations come together and help one another to grow wiser and harmonize the rights of individuals with other demands of social life..." (Vatican II: Church in the Modern World, #52).

for the one lost sheep. Jesus accepts the unacceptable and tells us that the Reign of God is within us. The Beatitudes exalt gentleness and mercy. The disciples are not to lord it over others as the pagans do. The Last Judgment rewards those who were attentive to the least of God's people. Forgiveness is seventy times seven.

Jesus washes the feet of those he leads. He calls his disciples friends rather than servants. Not law but charity is to be the hallmark of the Gospel. Women are given a prominent place in the circle of believers. Enemies are to be loved.

The memory of Christ, therefore, obliges the Church to respect the integrity of people and to allow as much individual authenticity as possible. The Church needs to impose certain guidelines and rules but also to find place for as much diversity as the community needs for its life.

The other basic elements of the Church combine authority and personal initiative. The Breaking of the Bread is a family celebration and yet there are rules to be followed. The elements of bread and wine, the words to be spoken, the faith meaning of the prayers and ritual, questions of presiding and speaking and assembly are stipulated. There is room for both spontaneity and formalism, for individual choice and prescribed procedures.

The Tradition of the Church has led it constantly in two directions. As the early Church grew and organized, it centralized its authority. Bishops and priests and deacons were given specific offices in the community, more or less modeled on the Roman pattern of government. The Church at Rome was accorded a special place in the

circle of Christian communities throughout the world. Sacramental rituals were developed. Creeds were formulated. Councils were convened.

At the same time, the Christian community saw itself as an assembly of believers, all of whom had a voice. Church officers were elected and Councils heard from laity as well as clerics. Theologians, later called "Fathers of the Church," offered different models for church government and theology, for the interpretation of Christ's words and the Spirit's direction of the Church. There was a great deal of diversity and option. In the midst of centralization, both collegiality and family remained important counterbalancing and moderating experiences.

Scripture, too, underwent the same process. In the early centuries, the Gospels and Epistles circulated freely through the community but with no hard and fast decisions as to which books were formally Scripture. Later a certain collection of the writings--the canon of Scripture, as it is called--was set. This need for an authoritative designation of the content of Scripture enables the Church to operate within a

(photo left)
The memory of Christ obliges the Church to respect the integrity of people and to allow as much individual authenticity as possible.

(photo below) "The world acquires flavor only when a little of the other world is mingled with it....The road to the sacred lies through the secular" (Abraham Heschel).

framework on which all are agreed. As a result, a common vocabulary and literature is established for all subsequent Church decision.

One can see, in all this, that the Church tries to hold two values in tension simultaneously. History has shown that the Church cannot survive as a unified body of believers unless some authority and order are operative. This authority benefits the community when it excludes leaders who might take advantage of people or guide them capriciously and exploit them. Such authority brings to each community of Christians a sense of the worldwide Church and of the heritage of that Church. It allows a consensus to emerge on who Christ is, what Scripture means, where Tradition leads us, how sacraments should be celebrated.

History also shows that authority can take advantage of the community and oppress it. It can become so centralized that all local and individual experiences are crushed or, at least, discounted. And so the Church allows discussion, disagreement and prophetic witness, personal gifts and new insights to flourish. This is done, not as a concession to those not in authority, but as a right of all God's people, as a counter-balance to the structured and official life of the Church, as a response to the Spirit who speaks through all the members of the Church. From this, the Church has gained resiliency and catholicity, durability and creativity, a respect for the dignity of people and for the inexhaustible content of the Christian message.

CONSCIENCE

The Catholic Church has taught consistently that conscience is the immediate norm for the guidance of our individual lives. Conscience is so important that we are not allowed to act against it even if it is mistaken.

There are, of course, qualifications and refinements in this position. Our conscience is expected to be an informed conscience, if we are responsible moral agents. We are not permitted to choose ignorance or indifference in the conduct of our personal lives. Nor must we use conscience as an excuse for whim, indulgence or selfishness.

We have no right, furthermore, to injure others or the community wrongfully in the exercise of conscience. When conscience is irresponsible, the community may protect itself by censure or correction.

Conscience has the potential of being the supreme and ultimate norm for our lives, an immediate, intimate and personal expression of God's will for us. For it to fulfill this role, however, it must act with integrity and care, with concern for the truth and sensitivity to the Gospel, with love of the community and respect for the rights of others.

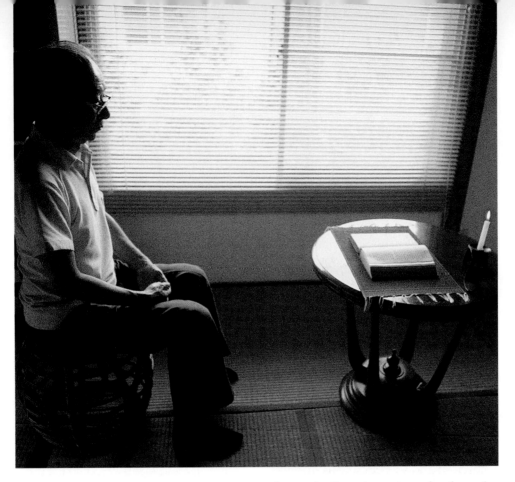

"Welcome the Word that has been planted in you..." (James 1:21).

Priorities and Roles

There are three areas for decision making which are most pivotal for the Church's life: *belief, behavior* and *order*. *Belief* is a statement of the teachings or truths the community considers most important for its life. *Behavior* is a code of ethical conduct, deriving from the belief system. *Order* is a series of decisions about how the community organizes its life and carries out its day-to-day activities.

An example may help here. A family has a *belief* system. This might include its acceptance of certain truths about marriage, its permanency or its purpose. A moral code might deal with sexual *behavior* or the use of money, or how anger is to be handled or whether social justice is a value for this family. *Order* would concern itself with issues such as attending family meals, proper attire in the house, rules for hospitality, responsibility for chores. One can see that the family would consider belief and moral decisions more important and would

change in these two areas slowly and deliberately if at all. Nonetheless, order is not unimportant to a family's life. Belief, behavior and order (or, discipline, as it is sometimes called) identify a community as profoundly as it is likely to be identified.

Two further aspects of this problem need to be addressed. One of these concerns priorities in each system.

Belief, for example, does not mean that a community or a family gives the same weight to all items in its belief scheme. Among the beliefs we recite in the Creed, the Trinity and the Incarnation count far more than the burial of Christ or the Ascension into heaven. It is not as though the latter issues are unimportant. The community, however, draws more of its life from the former doctrines.

The same concern with a hierarchy of values is present in moral decisions. The Church gives far more weight to its decisions about just wars, capital punishment or abortion than it does to decisions about consulting fortune tellers, disobeying parents or overeat-

(Apostles at Pentecost:) For Catholics, the ultimate sign of the Church's unity is the continued ministry of Peter found in the Papacy.

ing. All the issues have a point to them but they do not engage the Church's attention and life to the same degree.

Some disciplinary decisions of the Church—such as requiring celibacy for priests of the Latin rite or establishing the language of the Liturgy—influence the lives of people much more than Church decisions about the age of retirement for the clergy and the number of sponsors for Baptism.

We have, then, reached some important conclusions about authority in the Church. There needs to be an authority structure in the Church for the sake of its own life and order. The

structure is to be responsive and allow for participation and consultation as much as the message and memory of Jesus allow. This dynamic authority structure is especially important in matters of the community's belief, ethics and order.

We have one further problem to discuss. This concerns the designation of the offices and people in the Church who bear the most responsibility for decision-making. This process was rather easily settled in the first years of the Christian community. The original apostles and their witness were especially influential in guiding the community and in making decisions. Even here, however, it was possible for some later apostles, Paul, for example, who was not a member of the Twelve, to argue and dissent from judgments made by Peter, the leader of the Twelve. It was obvious also that the Twelve consulted the Church at large in assemblies or councils as a way of reaching a final decision.

After the initial generation of Christians passed from the scene, the community designated officers to have final decision-making authority. Eventually, these officers were called bishops. This conviction that bishops have the last word in Church discussion and debate has endured for centuries.

In choosing bishops for this role, the Church places the responsibility for its faith, ethics and discipline in those who are pastors in the Church rather than in those who are educators or theologians. Those in most immediate contact with the daily lives of people are those asked to formulate the Church's official positions. There is wisdom in this designation of pastoral leaders rather than others to perform this task, since care for people often makes us concrete and flexible in our thinking.

Bishops are expected to perform this role for the Church in synod, conference, or assembly with other bishops as well as alone in their own dioceses. They are to act in close contact with priests who share pastoral ministry with bishops and with deacons, laity and religious.

When all the bishops of the world meet in ecumenical council, the highest authority structure in the Church is put in place. These ecumenical councils have had more influence on the Church's belief, moral code and discipline than any other single factor.

For Catholics, the ultimate structural sign of the Church's unity is the Petrine ministry or the papacy. Catholics believe that the episcopate is unified in Peter's successor and that the Church is given a concrete and visible sign of oneness in a single person and office. Since so much is at stake in the papal leadership of the Church, Catholics are convinced that the Spirit is with the Bishop of Rome in a unique and effective manner. The infallibility of the Church finds expression in the papacy in a way that is different from its expression in other areas of Church life. The weight given to the papal office is considerable because it is likely that the one who has ultimate responsibility for the entire community will have a more comprehensive view of the Church. Such a person may, therefore, make decisions more responsibly and with sensitivity to the whole range of constituencies and traditions in the community.

"Only love constructs the world....How extraordinary the eloquence of Christ's question to Simon Peter by the lake of Galilee, 'Do you love me?' It is fundamental for all of us... 'Do you love?'" (Pope John Paul II).

7

MINISTRY AND SERVICE

There are those who maintain that the most impressive and significant ecumenical council ever assembled was the Second Vatican Council. This is, of course, difficult to prove since the history of the Church has been a long one, and there have been many other extraordinary and influential assemblies through the centuries. Some of those have had as their object a clear definition of who Christ is or a proper assessment of Mary in the liturgical, devotional, and theological life of believers. Other councils have sought to

"Every person ought to have ready access to all that is necessary for living a genuinely human life: food, clothing, housing...the right to education, to work, to his/her good name, to respect..." (Vatican II: Church in the Modern World, #26).

affirm the reality of Christ's presence in the Eucharist or to set the canon of Scripture.

We are, perhaps, too close to the Second Vatican Council (1962-1965) historically and too early in our task of developing its insights to have an accurate reading of all its intentions and impact. Nonetheless, there are some observations we can make, observations which, no doubt, will be made by later historians.

The Second Vatican council was the most global and international of Church assemblies and the largest ever held. All the continents of the world were represented and they were represented in substantial numbers. It was truly a catholic or universal meeting.

There had never been an ecumenical council which was so optimistic about the world and so intent on declaring

itself servant to the world for the sake of Christ. No council had given so positive and beautiful a description of marriage ("an intimate partnership of marital life and love"). No other council had taken the Church itself as the primary object of its attention or made so much of the laity.

The Council committed the Church to the reunion of all the divided Christian communities in the world, and it reformed the Liturgy with a simplicity and elegance that proved astonishing and inspiring. No council before it attempted to proclaim the goodness of those major world religions which were not Christian. Indeed, the catholicity and universality of the council was present not only in world-wide geographical representation but also in the range of its interests and documents.

tion. The Constitution on the Church is more than a theological treatise. It is a prolonged consideration of the Church as a mystery, and a celebration of the Church as a gift God has given us.

The document does not, of course, make the institutional structure of the Church unimportant. It could not do that and it did not wish to do that. It does, however, remind all believers that the Church is the People of God. The richness of this insight can hardly be exaggerated.

In chapter nine of this book, we shall explore other implications and interpretations of the Second Vatican Council. In this chapter, however, we wish to develop the image, ''People of God,'' as it refers to new concepts of ministry and service.

People of God

The reality of the Church is so enriched and profound that no one image can exhaust its reality. Indeed, the Church may be best perceived by considering all its differing images in tension with one another. Nonetheless, the Second Vatican Council was convinced that the image *People of God* had a special relevance for this time in history and for this particular council.

The image is biblical, and it links the Church with Israel, which saw itself as the People of God, as well as with the early Christian community which believed it was God's People in Christ.

The image, furthermore, suggests an emphasis not on structure but on people. We know, of course, that these terms are not exclusive and that, indeed, they are complementary. A people needs to organize itself for the

(photo left) "If we find the job where we can be of use, we are hitched to the star of the world and move with it" (Richard Cabot).

Suffice it to say that there are reasons to support the claim that the Second Vatican Council may have been the most impressive and significant, perhaps the most creative, ecumenical council ever assembled. The Council was the only one to be convoked, not to meet a crisis, but to reflect and meditate, to contemplate and review the work of the Church and its nature. It was, as though, at the end of two millennia of history, the Church wished to assess where it had been and what its future might be.

The first document of the Second Vatican Council in order of importance and the first in the collection of conciliar documents is the Constitution on the Church, ''The Light of the Nations'' or **Lumen Gentium** in its official Latin designa-

The gifts of ministry are contained in the life of the community. To all believers, Christ gives a mission. The Gospel is not to be placed in our hands and kept there.

husband is not less than a wife, and, yet, who would maintain that child and parent, husband and wife are indistinguishable?

And, so, in the Church, we are equal in terms of Baptism and discipleship. No one member of the Church is less baptized than another to be a disciple of Christ in the fullest meaning of that term. It is this equality in Baptism and discipleship which forms the basis for a renewed theology of ministry and service. Baptism, as we have seen, is a sacrament of priesthood, making us a holy nation, a people set apart. It is, furthermore, a sacrament which gives us access to the Eucharist, which is the central sacrament of the Church and at the very core of its being. This access includes full participation in Eucharist and full communion in the Body of Christ. No baptized person at a Eucharistic celebration is less than any other, including the ordained celebrant, in relationship to partaking of the mystery of Christ's Presence.

Each disciple, furthermore, is called to be a total disciple. This vocation or calling comes from God who summons us in the Spirit so that we might participate fully in the Church and so that we might bring Christ to the world. All believers are meant to be as completely as possible ecclesial persons, no less the Church than any other, including that disciple who serves the Church in the papal ministry. Each disciple, including the Pope, is invited to encounter the mystery of Christ's Church entirely and to share in all its sacramentality.

And, yet, in this radical and fundamental equality, there are clear, useful and desirable differences. Some of the baptized are called to preside or to

sake of its unity and its permanence in history. Nonetheless, the intent of the Second Vatican Council was to stress a theology of the Church which made people and community a prime consideration. The image, finally, envisions the assembly of God's People in terms of its equality. This equality does not mean that differences, uniqueness, diversity, and degrees of responsibility are discounted. We are, for example, all equal in our humanity, and yet we do not all have the same roles or function with the same measure of authority. We are, to cite another example, all equal in terms of our membership in our respective families and yet, within that family, all are not assigned the same place. A child is not less a member of the family than a parent, a

"In the sacred books, God who is in heaven comes lovingly to meet his children, and talks with them" (cf. *Vatican II: Divine Revelation, #21).*

"To work is to pray"
(St. Benedict).

preach, to organize or to witness, to teach or to heal, to live in marital community or celibate love or the single life. Not all are called to the same task, and no one is allowed to exercise each and every ministry. Some of the disciples have gifts of social justice or theology, of administration or spiritual guidance, of financial management or music, of counseling or writing, of liturgical planning or hospital chaplaincy. Each disciple affirms a ministry and allows another to flourish.

Many Gifts, One Ministry

The gifts of ministry are contained in the life of the community. To all believers, Christ gives a mission. The Gospel is not to be placed in our hands and kept there. To all the baptized, Christ imparts priesthood. We might distinguish, as later theology and Church teaching do, between common and ordained priesthood. Indeed, this is a distinction both laity and clergy prefer to make because each chooses to play a different role in the Church. Such a distinction prevails also in Protestant communities where a pastor is brought into the community's life with different rituals, ceremonies, calling and authority.

Nonetheless, the preference at the Second Vatican Council, and even more forcefully in the years since that Council, is in the direction of affirming the unity between lay ministers and ordained ministry.

Baptism is the focal point of that unity since all the baptized are priests in some way and since all priests, including the ordained, must be baptized. Baptism brings both lay and ordained Christians to the Eucharist for the fulfillment of their Baptism and priesthood. All authority in ministry and Church is rooted, sacramentally, in the Baptism we share. Baptism prepares one for mission and ministry.

The Second Vatican Council took as one of its central themes the doctrine of collegiality. Collegiality on one level of the Church's life means that the bishops govern and teach in the Church in union with their elder brother bishop, the pope, and that the ministry of pope and bishop is meant to be harmonized. Since the Council, this collegial principle has been extended, though in modified form, by the official Church to include priests and bishops together in each diocese, represented by presbyterial councils or priests' senates. Likewise, within the parish, laity, associates and pastor together make up the parish council or team.

This collegial principle is rooted in the nature of the Church, which is a community or family, and in the nature of Baptism, which is a sacrament of unity and equality.

All ministry, then, lay and ordained, comes from the community, from its collegial life, from its shared Baptism, from its common priesthood. To be a Christian is to have a mission and a ministry.

St. Paul identified all believers as members of Christ's body. Since Christ is preeminently the model of mission and ministry, we all share in this aspect of his life.

Just as a human body, though it is made up of many parts, is a single unit because all those parts, though many, make up one body, so it is with Christ. In the one Spirit, we were all baptized, Jews as well as Greeks, slaves as well as citizens, and one Spirit was given to us all... Now you together are Christ's body; but each of you is a different part of it... (I Corinthians 12:12-13,27).

Ministry and Service

There is an important item to add to what we have said thus far. The Church is not only a mystery and a sacrament, a people called by God, a

"The best things are nearest: breath in your nostrils, light in your eyes, flowers at your feet, duties at your hand, the path of God just before you" (Robert L. Stevenson).

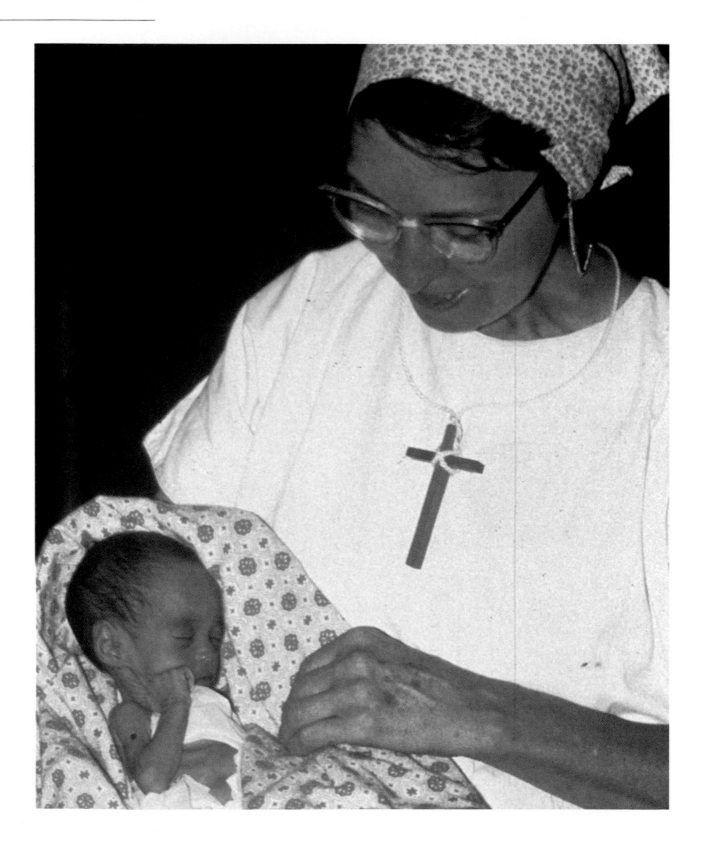

body of believers who follow the Gospel and are led by the Spirit. It is also an organized community and it was this from the very beginning.

The memory of Christ has not been left to the community at large only but depends, for the most part, on the witness of the apostles. The Liturgy has not been dependent on personal and arbitrary choices but is given a structured form by the Church. Tradition is not established in whatever people choose to do in the name of Christ. Tradition must evolve from the whole Church, official and unofficial, for it to

have a permanent place in the community's life. The canon of Scripture was not set by local communities of scattered Christians but emerged over the centuries, proclaimed by the Church's pastoral leaders as normative.

It is, therefore, imperative that ministry also be organized within the Church. No community lasts long or functions with unity if it allows absolutely anything to be done. The memory of Christ would become a confused memory if all actions of the community were given the same

(photo left) "Right living is like a work of art, the product of a vision and of a wrestling with concrete situations" (Abraham Heschel).

SACRAMENTAL MINISTRY

Some of the Church's memories of Jesus are rooted in contemplation, some in the Word, some in sacrament. Although contemplation may be the deepest experience and memory of Jesus, the Church as an institution does not, for the most part, become involved in legislating about this aspect of Christian life. Contemplation is so much in the private sphere of a person's life that there would be no way to intrude in this without disrupting it.

As the memory of Jesus becomes more verbal, however, more intimately connected with Scripture and Liturgy, with the teaching and preaching Christ, the official Church takes a more active part. This is because the Word binds others and influences them and declares the identity and definition of the Church in the public order. Even here, however, most of our words about Christ are not official teachings. Though unofficial, these words may be not only profound words but may be the best words used of Christ. Since they are not proclaimed in a context of official Church teaching, these words are left to the community's sense of Christ rather than to authoritative and official review.

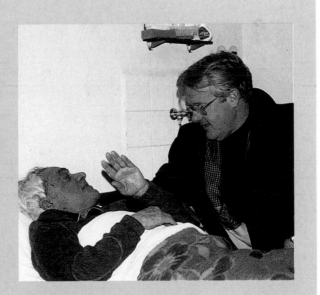

It is the memory of Christ in sacrament where the Church believes its life and structure are most intensely and publicly committed. There are no private sacraments, so to speak, no informal or unofficial sacraments. Sacrament, of its very nature, is an official action of the Church, one which comes from the core of the Church's life and engages it profoundly and publicly. It is in this area that the official Church is most active in reviewing and certifying those ministers who conduct such worship.

The Church is about creating communities of believers throughout the world. The entire Church is present in the parish community's expression of it.

weight, if none was evaluated, judged, corrected or approved.

If all are called to ministry or service, not all ministries are official ministries in the Church. There is another dimension to ministry which is important, namely, the Church's recognition of it and official approbation of it.

A process of recognition and ratification is deemed imperative not only by Catholics but also by Protestants who assume official ministries only with the assent and proper commissioning of their respective communities.

The more deeply the ministry in question involves the life of the Church and influences it, the more necessary it is that this ministry receive proper endorsement. Such ministries require more accountability to others, longer periods of training,

and are subject to extensive review. This aids not only the Church but also the minister by giving such a person community support and by leading the minister to a more comprehensive view of the life of the Church and of the needs of the community.

Ministries which are not official are a form of Christian service. Thus, a mother may love her children and teach them the Gospel, or a social activist might give Christian witness, or a physician may conduct his practice compassionately. These activities may be done in virtue of Baptism and discipleship so that they have a sacramental, evangelical and ecclesial dimension to them. They are done in the name of Christ and are, therefore, Christian to the core. They build up the Body of Christ.

Yet there is something about them which does not require official recognition. There are two reasons why this is not necessary. In the first instance, these forms of service are so constant and varied in their structure that to impose upon them an order which would require recognition and approval through official Church procedures and representatives would destroy them. Love and personal teaching about Christ, care for one's neighbor, and moral living must be affirmed by the Church in less official and cumbersome ways.

There are, however, other ministries which need to be ordered if the Church is to function in the world as an organized community. The Liturgy and preaching, the proclamation of Scripture, and the music which informs worship, the public teaching of doctrinal and moral norms, the sacramental care of the sick, or counseling in the name of the Church, these and other ministries identify the Church formally and commit the Church as a community.

It is useful and desirable, therefore, that there be for such ministries a process of review and approval.

This approbation of the official Church is not incidental or secondary, unnecessary or intrusive. The official minister's calling does come from Baptism and discipleship, but these realities orient one toward the community and come about only because there is a community to baptize and to preach Christ. The formal designation of ministers by the Church, therefore, is an intimate dimension of Christian ministry.

Official ministry is different from Christian service. Christian service tends to be a more spontaneous response to the Spirit. Since the person need not consider all the implications of certain actions in terms of involving the entire Church, so to speak, the person can act more freely and readily. Most of the Church's life must remain "unofficial" if the Church is to be a true community of persons rather than a juridical structure. If we call attention to every action of a believer, leaving nothing to the person, the vitality of life itself would be destroyed.

All Christian service is baptismal and ecclesial, but only some of it is official ministry. If all were official, as we have said, the official Church would be intrusive and would have little regard for the spirit-inspired or unstructured aspects of the Church's life.

Official ministry is not more than unofficial service but each is different. What is important is that both are ministry. The Church lives by all the deeds and words of its members. A

"O Lord, your kindness reaches to heaven; your faithfulness to the clouds.... For with you is the fountain of life, and in your light we see light"
(Psalm 36:6,10).

family functions in the same manner.

Love is the heart of the Church, but love as such is not official even though some of its manifestations may be.

8

PARISH AND COMMUNITY

I t is in the parish that the reality of the universal Church affects people most concretely. It is in the parish that this Church which has endured for two thousand years and developed through millennia of human history comes into the lives of present-day believers.

All the original elements in the Church are given expression in one's own neighborhood. Now it is one's own friends and associates who remember Christ, one's own family, perhaps, who participate in the Eucharist as

"So, as you received Christ Jesus the Lord, walk in him, rooted in him and built upon him and established in faith as you were taught, abounding in thanksgiving" (Colossians 2:6-7).

ministers. Now the spirit of the Church's Tradition reaches into the lives of those whose faces and names we know. Now we ourselves hear the Church's Scripture read once more as it has been for centuries.

All the essential features of the Church's life reach us in a community whose members we know and whose pastoral leaders know us. This community is not a local branch of a large multi-national organization. It is a community which embodies in its life all the central dynamism of the universal Church's life. Into this community, Christ and Liturgy, Tradition and Scripture exist as fully as they do

anywhere else in the world. This community helps to shape the universal Church. If its influence seems to be modest, it is nonetheless real.

The universal Church is not managed by the papacy in such a manner that all dioceses and parishes are merely the agents of policy coming from Rome. Rather, the universal Church is a circle of dioceses and parishes, each of which is complete in itself, even if not fully autonomous, and all of which have the Bishop of Rome as a central, unifying influence.

Family of Faith

Christianity is always at its best when it is reduced to human proportions. Small communities of Christians, in each and every instance, is what all the massiveness of the universal Church seeks to accomplish. The Church is about creating communities of believers throughout the World. The entire Church is present in the parish community's expression of it.

Enduring questions and continuing challenges also make themselves felt. In the parish, all the sacraments are celebrated and with a regularity and commitment which make this little community a fully sacramental one. Christians are continually initiated into the mystery of Christ and of the Church's faith in Christ by Baptism, Confirmation and Eucharist. Those who are troubled are anointed and reconciled; the marriages of believers are celebrated; and ministry is exercised by the community's ordained and lay pastoral leaders.

As these sacraments are solemnized, all the drama and richness of Christ's life are reenacted, all the life stages and commitments of a believer's life

are engaged, all the long history of the Church's journey through time is symbolized, all that this local community seeks to become is realized and proclaimed.

In this small community of families and friends, Christ is born again and the Spirit is given, Bread is broken as it was at the Last Supper, and the ministry of Jesus is continued as the sick and the repentant are healed.

In this parish, marriage becomes a mystery in which Christ's love for the Church is given expression. The intimate partnership of marital life and love, which marriage is, reminds the community of how intense and total love can be and of how faithful and self-giving Christ's love for us is.

In this small body of believers, the priesthood is given once more, not only as a common gift for all the baptized, not only in the official ministry and Christian service to which believers are called, but also in that special, pastoral role which sacramental ordination confers.

The parish celebrates Christmas so that Jesus will be welcomed in the inn of this little community and not left again with no place to go. In this parish, the feet of our fellow disciples are washed, and the awful reality of the cross is raised into our consciousness. In this parish, all the meditative power of Advent waiting and Lenten sacrifice, all the faith values of parables and miracles, all the fortifying force of the Spirit's descent upon us and of our mission to the world are made part of our lives. This parish prays and sings the Easter Vigil every year so that Christ, when he is risen once more, will find a community of believers awaiting him in the upper room where we gather.

Here, too, intimately and persuasively, our consciences are formed and the apostolic authority of the Church is encountered. As we struggle with faith and ethics, with life style and devotion, the Church seeks to harmonize our choices and decisions with the message of Jesus as it understands it. Our conscience is meant to be not only a personal guide but a Christian conscience. The authority of the Church is not only universal but it has a specific application in the practical lives of believers. In a parish setting, fidelity to Church teachings can be presented with the pastoral sensitivity and resiliency which can only happen when people are addressed face to face and when all the particular circumstances of their lives are taken into account.

"To maintain a joyful family requires much. ...Each one must show concern, not only for his or her own life, but also for the lives of other members of the family: their needs, their hopes, their ideals" (John Paul II).

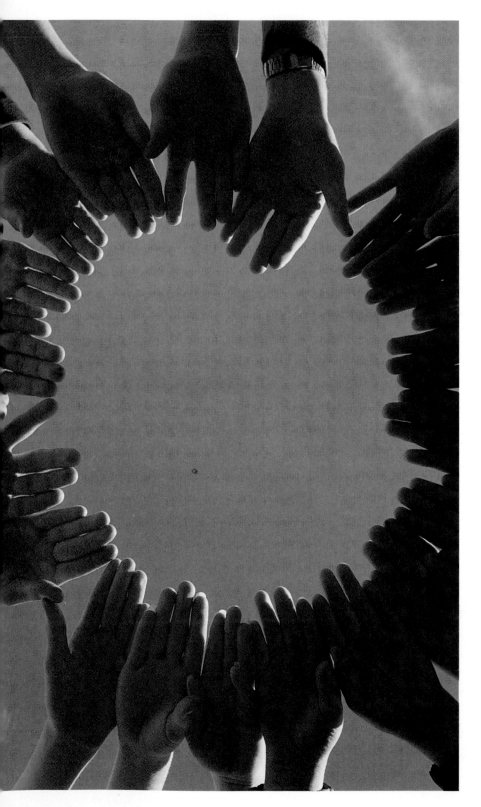

And so the parish is a marvelous place to be, a community whose meaning and life are inexhaustible, a Christian event of the first order. In the parish community, there are often memories of one's own Baptism and wedding day, of the funeral services for one's family members, of First Communion and Confirmation, of times when all one's sins were absolved, and of liturgies which celebrated the entire range of a parish's memorable anniversaries and achievements.

The parish community assembles the young and the elderly, the intelligent and the bewildered, the newly married and the recently divorced, the children just baptized, the widows and the wanderers, the troubled in heart and those still bold in their faith, the grief stricken and the exuberant. As these gifts and experiences, as these sorrows and joys are meshed and intertwined, a rich community of life is created.

From this parish community, the Spirit summons ministers so that the needs of these believers and of people at large may be served. Some of this ministry will be official, but all of it will be enriched Christian service if the Spirit is allowed to accomplish its life in us. A Christian community is not only a community of memories but one of mission, not only a liturgical assembly but a ministerial resource, not only a gathering of the Church's Tradition but one of sensitivity and compassion, not only a place for Scripture to be proclaimed but the place where it is implemented and lived.

In all of this, we can see that the parish community is a synthesis of all that we have been dealing with from the first chapter of this book. It is a synthesis which is not academic or theological but a synthesis which is concrete and personal, experiential and immediate. In the parish, one beholds the Church and encounters the Church. It is as simple and as profound as that.

The parish community binds together all the essential elements of the Church's life and it invites us to live them. The Church is not to be admired or organized, observed or analyzed. It is not an ideology but a life. It is to be lived and loved. It is to be participated in and made our own.

The parish gives us the opportunity, then, to engage Christ directly in a community and sacramental setting and to encounter the Church concretely in a personal and immediate relationship. This gives us an extraordinary opportunity for meditation and contemplation.

Contemplative Love in Community

There are differing ways to consider what may be the end result of all our

striving and faith, of all our efforts with the Church and our experiences with Christ. It is worth affirming that contemplative love in community may be the final object of human life. These few words, ''contemplative love in community,'' imply and presuppose a great deal.

The first observation we might make about such a description is that it ought not be mistaken for individual-

(photos left and above) "The larger and richer our community, the larger and richer is the content of self. There is no individuality without community" (Madeleine L'Engle).

CONTEMPLATION

Contemplation is not an exotic experience. It is a reflective and serene meditation on where our lives are going and to whom they are account-able. Contemplation may happen as we listen to music or watch a snowfall, as we drive alone in a car or wait in a physician's office. We need only think about ourselves, in life review, and then about others in our relationships. We find, as we do this, that questions of meaning and purpose, memories of joy and regret crowd our minds. It is not a difficult step to include God in all this and to pray in love for all that needs yet to be done and for all we have been given.

(photo right) "Our Lord does not care so much for the importance of our works as for the love with which they are done" (Teresa of Avila).

ism, isolation, subjectivism, self-indulgence. For some people, such words might be seen as an invitation to retreat from the painful but creative tasks of social justice in the world or reform and renewal in the Church.

A Christian is obliged, clearly by the words of Jesus and by the breaking of bread, to care about the hungry and the homeless, the impoverished and disadvantaged, the vulnerable and the oppressed. This care is not to be only a passing thought for those who suffer or a prayer on their behalf. It is to be more than a concern with this or that person. It is to be a commitment to change the basic structures in society which violently deprive human beings of their humanity, the substance of their lives, and their very hope.

A Christian is obliged to this task, not only by the words of Jesus and the breaking of bread, as we have said, but also by the heart of the Church's Tradition and the core of the biblical message.

The Spirit impels us to confront those organized and apparently invincible institutions which brutally diminish and destroy human lives. Political and military, educational and corporate, economic and social structures sometimes function with callous disregard for human values. They become, at times, insensitive to the human cost of maintaining such organizations and to the long range suffering and even destruction caused by their drive for power and profit.

GOD HAS THE LAST WORD

Greek dramatists tell us that one's virtue is often one's vice. Courage, for example, can easily become arrogance; patience might lead to indifference.

One of the greatest virtues of American culture is its energy and efficiency. One of its disabilities may be its assumption that human action and planning, organization and skill can accomplish almost anything. We easily overlook the fact that our best efforts in one area sometimes create problems in another.

The message of the Gospel is extremely important for Americans in this regard. An American Catholic is not to be someone who abandons the virtues of our culture but someone who tempers them with a realism which rescues us from excess and frenzy. Human effort is both necessary and dangerous. It leads us to active and effective engagement with problems but it be-

guiles us into thinking we can solve more human problems than we can.

One of the most heartbreaking experiences in life is the discovery that even when everything seems to have gone right and been done correctly, the final result is not successful.

"Contemplative love in community" assures us that the last word in human and ecclesial life is God's Word and that the Presence of God is the core and the heart of all our striving.

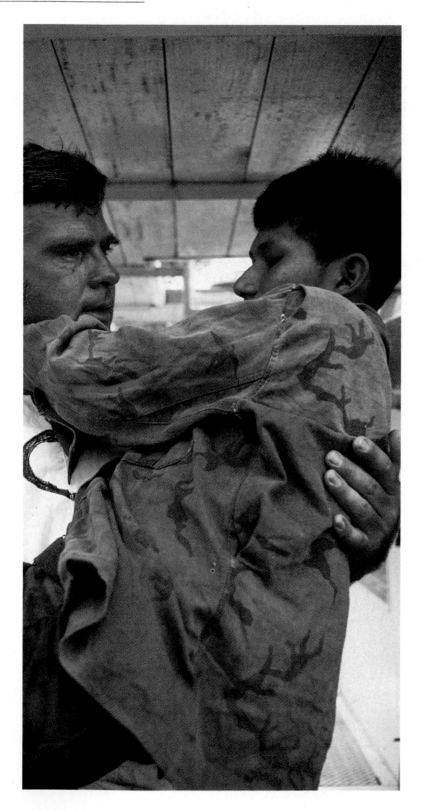

"Contemplative love in community" is not an objective for the Church if the element of social justice has been neglected. A Christian has no warrant to worship God and favor nuclear war or to celebrate Liturgy and prefer an unjust economic system.

"Contemplative love in community" obliges us, furthermore, to develop community in the life of the Church. Community is the greatest of our deeds, since it implies all the Christian values. It is also the most demanding.

Community formation, however, requires that we deal with and are even shaped by those with whom we do not always agree. Certainly, ecumenism and interreligious dialogue are part of this endeavor. Even in the exclusively Catholic membership of a community, there are conservatives and liberals, preservers of the former values and formulators of new visions. There are temperaments and theologies, different goals and diversified gifts. All of this needs to be addressed and reconciled for genuine community to happen.

The community must be as universal as possible in its scope. Small communities are sometimes frozen on a level of like-mindedness or at a certain socio-economic stratum. They are often made up of people who have the same racial or ethnic culture. This frequently limits access to the group even when not intended. On the other hand, the strength of small communities lies in their capacity to allow people to meet face-to-face, to be known by name and to be loved precisely for who they are.

The parish has the capacity to gather small communities and to keep their liabilities to a minimum while magnifying their assets. The parish

"...the fruit of the Spirit is love, joy, peace, patience, kindness, generosity, faithfulness, gentleness, self-control" *(Galatians 5:22).*

(photo left) "Christianity taught us to care. Caring is the greatest thing. Caring matters most" (Friedrich Von Hugel).

welcomes and embraces people from all aspects of human life. To make community out of this heterogeneity and diversity is a difficult, demanding but desirable goal.

As we deal with "contemplative love in community" as a goal for the Church, we are not proposing that people become irresponsible or indulgent, evasive and withdrawn, self-centered or indolent.

Why, then, do we propose this ideal as perhaps the end result of the Church's life?

We do this because we believe that the encounter with God is the central focus of the religious life of the Church. It is God, encountered with all the love for our brothers and sisters that includes, who finally settles us and fully rejoices us. Our restless hearts do not ultimately repose in a world of justice or even in a Church without blemish. We have, quite simply, been made for God.

It is especially important that Americans be kept aware of this. The glory of American life is often in the practical activity it expends in the pursuit of its ideals. The defect in American life is the illusion that practical action and efficient activity can resolve almost all problems. We, Americans, most particularly, must come to understand that "contemplative love in community" is the essence of the Church's life.

The purpose of the remembrance of Christ, of the Liturgy, of the Tradition of the Church and Scripture, of sacramental symbols and faith affirmation, of moral norms and disciplinary choices, of all ministry and parish life is the silence and wonder which settles us as we become aware that God is all. It is clear that this contemplative response is linked with social justice and community. But it is also important to realize that this contemplative response is essential, fulfilling and irreplaceable.

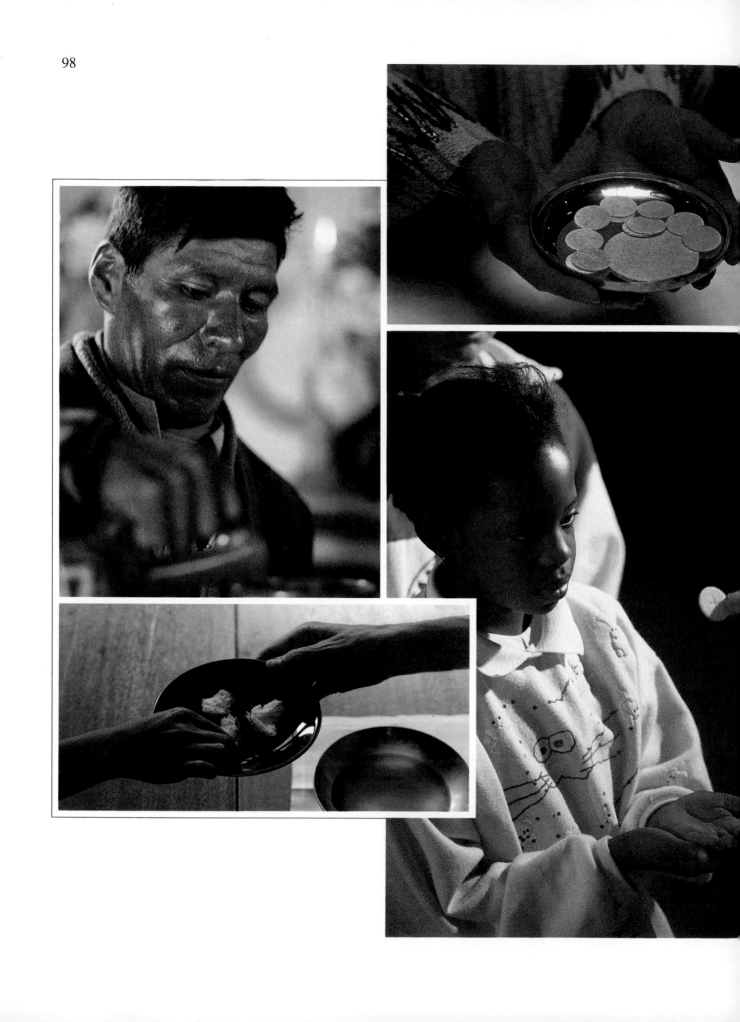

"As often as the sacrifice of the cross by which 'Christ, our Pasch is sacrificed' (*1 Corinthians* 5:7) is celebrated on the altar, the work of our redemption is carried out. Likewise, in the sacrament of the Eucharistic bread, the unity of believers, who form one body in Christ (cf. *1 Corinthians* 10:17), is both expressed and brought about. All are called to this union with Christ, who is the light of the world, from whom we go forth, through whom we live, and towards whom our whole life is directed.

"...the Church, in Christ, is in the nature of a sacrament—a sign and instrument, that is, of communion with God and of unity among all people..."

adapted from
Vatican Council II 1964
DOGMATIC CONSTITUTION ON THE CHURCH *IV:32*

III. ENDURING QUESTIONS: CONTINUING CHALLENGES

9

CATHOLIC IDENTITY

The future of Christianity is inextricably linked with Catholicism. This statement does not imply that Orthodoxy or Protestantism do not have a significant contribution to make. Nor does it exclude those many witness and reform movements throughout history, some considered schismatic or heretical and others merely left to wither on the margins of Church life, which have brought about abiding changes in Catholicism.

It is a matter of historical record, a record which transcends all theoretical formulations

The community is always under the influence of the Spirit and so its Tradition is not only a repetition of its past but a powerful creative force in the present.

of the Church, that the Catholic Tradition has endured longer and, indeed, includes most of the Christian world. No other Christian Tradition has achieved identifiable structural form for so long a time and so clearly over the centuries.

This impressive and unique phenomenon, massive in its sheer number of years and in its accumulation of members, cannot be seriously discounted. One might even conclude, somewhat boldly, that there never has been and, perhaps, never will be a Christian form of Church more successful than that achieved by Catholicism.

If one affirms all this, there yet remain other, less positive statements to consider.

There is, for example, the danger that such assertions sound triumphalistic. There is the peril that Catholics may be so enamored of their faith history that they begin to see the Church as a human achievement, which hardly needs God. They may see the Church as a measurable success which assumes that truth has some essential connection with numbers and longevity. These temptations are especially attractive to American Catholics.

There is, furthermore, a tendency in all of this for Catholics to overlook the sins of the Church and the wounds, the shame and the guilt which must also be recognized. The Church, in the words of the Second Vatican Council, is a pilgrim people, an assembly of believers always in need of repentance and reform, a community of disciples who require renewal from God's Spirit.

The Church must constantly proclaim the courage of its convictions and the boldness of its faith that God is ultimately and infallibly with it. It must also continually beg for pardon since its heart has not been free from blemish.

The Orthodox and Protestant alternatives to Catholicism are the two most successful and long-lived of all those communities which have affirmed their faith in such a way that it led to a rejection of Roman Catholicism. It would be myopic to imply that these alternative Churches get all their identification merely from the fact that they are ''non-catholic'' or that the energy which drives them is resistance to the Catholic system. This would be

世界人類が平和でありますように

MAY PEACE PREVAIL ON EARTH

(photo left) "*With loyalty to the Gospel.... the Church, whose duty it is to foster and elevate all that is true, all that is good, and all that is beautiful in the human community, consolidates peace among all people for the glory of God*" *(cf. Vatican II: Church in Modern World, #76).*

nobility and authority of the laity and the crucial role of Scripture in the life of the Church are rich resources for all Christians. These values must have required more development than they were given in Catholicism at one time or else the alternative Churches would not have seemed so right to the millions of Catholics who joined them. The Second Vatican Council recognized the need for these changes and moved the Catholic Church in their direction.

This is not to say, however, that Catholicism does not have the ability to take these values of other Churches even further. Collegiality, for example, may function better when balanced with papacy. Lay life might be enriched when an enhanced authority is given to ordained pastors. Scripture may be strengthened as it is interpreted through Tradition and proclaimed with a decisive teaching voice.

In any case, it may well be futile and even lead to a form of ecumenical paralysis to try any longer to determine how all this came about, who is to blame and which Church has been right. A divided Christian family is a scandal and a heart-ache as is any shattered family. It could not have been the intention of Jesus that we would end up like this. He prayed on the night before his death that all his disciples who heard his voice and loved him would be united.

It may well serve the cause of ecumenism better and indeed advance the cause of Christ if each Church declares what it is in itself, not in relationship to alternative Churches, nor even in terms of past disagreements, but in its present understanding of what it means to be faithful to Christ, now, in its own Tradition.

not only a narrow but a pernicious reading of history. The alternative Churches achieve their significance, under grace, and by the development of those creative energies which enable them to be what they are.

The Orthodox and Protestant experiments may well have been created, in part, by the failure of Catholicism to attend to elements of the Christian Tradition which were being neglected or to the needs of people which were urgent. Catholicism may well be incomplete until it acquires from these other Churches those very values which remain underdeveloped in Catholicism.

The Orthodox emphasis, for example, on the collegiality of bishops and the decisive character of each bishop's ministry in the local Church or the Protestant insistence on the

The sacramental system is an endless celebration of Christ. Catholics have emphasized the radical innocence of the baptized and reconciled, the essential goodness of human institutions and church structures, the basic decency of the human family.

Perhaps the most difficult and demanding of the questions confronting Catholicism today is the concern with defining what it is to be Catholic. There are millions of Catholics who struggle with this question, a question at the heart of our loyalties, our ecumenical sensitivities, our involvement in the contemporary moment in which we live. Let us, therefore, attempt an answer.

Sacramentality

There is, perhaps, no feature of Catholic life which has a greater hold on the identity and spirituality of Catholics than the sacramental system. It is, perhaps, Catholicism's most creative contribution to the Christian Tradition. This sacramentality has led the Catholic Church to organize itself around the Eucharistic Liturgy and to offer its members the sacramental presence of Christ as the deepest sign of their acceptance by Christ and the Church.

Sacramentality has inspired the Catholic community to offer the sacraments of Anointing and Reconciliation so regularly that a minister who does either of these is assumed by all to be Catholic. The Church has provided for its future sacramentally, not only with the Baptism of its members (which, of course, all Christian Churches affirm) but with the identification of Marriage and Orders as sacraments, an identification made by almost no other Christian Church.

Sacramental roots are so deep in the Catholic consciousness that Christ is proclaimed as a sacrament of God and the Church itself as a sacrament of Christ. These sacramental affinities are so persuasive for Catholics that the Church feels closest to those Christian Churches whose sacramental life has been most developed.

This sacramentality has led Catholicism to become embodied in the world and in humanity the way few, if any, Churches have been. Since sacraments are physical and tangible realities, the intensive adherence of the Church to these sacraments has enabled it to feel very much at home in the world and to create a Church which claims more for its human structures than any other Church does.

The Catholic Church has a tendency not only to yearn for the Reign of God but to delight in the world the human family has made. It declared this better than ever in the Council's Pastoral Constitution on the Church in the Modern World. In that document, it celebrated the contemporary world with an exuberance which was not uncritical but which was remarkably optimistic.

Authority

Although the Catholic Church has been distinctive in the intensity and frequency of its celebration of sacraments, most of its energy goes into other facets of Church life. These would include works of love and social justice, teaching and organization, counseling and prayer. The Catholic Church is also distinguishable by its orientation to the question of authority. And, yet, its members are more energetically committed to the life of their own conscience.

There has never been a Christian community of any significant size and duration which has not built authority structures into its system. These structures are already implied in the original elements of the Church since the memory of Christ is not just anyone's memory but a memory residing in the apostles. The Breaking of the Bread is not done arbitrarily, but requires an agreed-upon ritual and an acceptable celebrant. Tradition is not made up of anything the Christian community chooses to do but only of those deeds which are in accord with the nature of the Church and which are done with this conviction. Scripture is written and compiled and, finally, given official status and interpretation by those whom the community accepts as having the authority to do this.

"We are made for prayer, 'programmed' for it, just as we are made to speak our own language. We all have a contemplative core that needs to be developed in prayer" (Segundo Galilea).

The sacramental system we have just considered requires authoritative decisions about how many sacraments there are, who is to perform the rituals, under which circumstances, and what these sacraments mean. The question of authority is, therefore, an unavoidable one.

The Catholic Church gives unique authority to ecumenical councils. These are Church assemblies which, over the centuries, have had bishops as their core voting members and include the Bishop of Rome as an essential voice in the final public teaching of faith, ethics and discipline. The history of the Church has been one in which bishops have been considered the final voice in Church matters, but not without substantial consultation with laity and religious, theologians and priests.

There have been other Christian churches which have accepted ecumenical councils and the episcopate as guides for the development of their official positions. There has been only one Christian Church which envisions the whole body of bishops as dynamically oriented toward the papacy. The

ATTENTIVE LISTENING

The Latin root of the word "obedience" does not imply that one do what one is told, but that one listen attentively to what is said. "Obedient" comes from the Latin word "to hear."

The word "absurd" means etymologically that one is "deaf." These two words are useful in trying to understand how Catholicism is meant to influence the lives of believers.

A Catholic is someone always "obedient" to the Church, always listening attentively to its Liturgy and Scripture, its sacramental proclamation and official teaching, its optimism and spirituality, its struggle to express its comprehensiveness. A Catholic is never meant to be "deaf" to the Church so that the Church is "absurd" and unheard.

We do not preclude by this distinction the fact that there are times when a Catholic is expected to follow directions. All Churches require this on occasion. The full range of Catholic "obedience," however, is attentive listening. This implies that the Word is always shaping us and that we are open to change and dialogue.

For those of us who are contemporary Catholics, no Church experience can quite match the

sense of obedience we feel to the Second Vatican Council. Never perhaps was the Church more visibly comprehensive, more "obedient," so to speak, to its members and to Christ, to the other Churches and religions and to the world at large. Because the Church heard so well, it spoke magnificently and made "obedience" a joy and a grace to experience.

papacy is the most distinct authoritative structure in Catholicism. Indeed, it is defined by Catholics as capable of expressing the infallibility of the Church if a number of crucial conditions are met. This papacy is bound to the collegial government of the Church and to Tradition and Scripture. It functions always within the boundaries of apostolic witness. Yet it has a decisiveness and finality which no other authority structure in the Catholic Church possesses.

The Catholic Church gives considerable weight, furthermore, to what is technically called the ''magisterium.'' This is the cumulative teaching of bishops and assemblies of bishops and, of course, that of the papacy. This magisterium sets guidelines and official policy, doctrine and moral norms.

When authority functions best, it allows an order and universality, indeed, a climate of toleration and dialogue to develop. It gives a Church solidity and endurance.

Authority, however, like all things human, is liable to abuse. The Catholic Church seeks to forestall this by the appeal of the community to collegiality and conscience and by continual reference to the original basic elements of Church.

Optimism and Service

The ministry of the Church over the centuries has been developed with a strong emphasis on optimism. Catholics have emphasized that evil has no final hold on this community, nor does error. The memory of Christ prevails, the Breaking of the Bread is constant, the forgiveness of sins is proclaimed.

This Community is always under

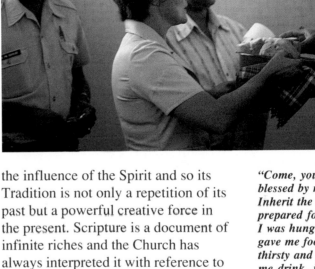

the influence of the Spirit and so its Tradition is not only a repetition of its past but a powerful creative force in the present. Scripture is a document of infinite riches and the Church has always interpreted it with reference to contemporary life and not in a rigid or literal manner.

The sacramental system is an endless celebration of Christ. Authority has served the Church well in its long history or the Church would not have endured with so much venerability and force, life and creativity.

Catholics have emphasized the radical innocence of the baptized and reconciled, the essential goodness of human institutions and Church structures, the basic decency of the human family. The Catholic Church is a Church of ceremony and celebration, a Church convinced it is indestructible and one which has proven its invincibility through the centuries, sometimes against incredible odds.

The Catholic spirit does not encourage brooding over sin or darkness. It has managed to be very much at home

"Come, you who are blessed by my Father. Inherit the Reign prepared for you....For I was hungry and you gave me food, I was thirsty and you gave me drink...in prison and you visited me" (cf. Matthew 25:34-36).

in the world and yet clearly defined as a community whose strength and vision come from another Source. It is able to live in all the cultures of the world and yet somehow manages to transcend them.

Spirituality and Community

The Catholic Church has made a more intensive effort than any other Christian community to systematize and create a theology of the spiritual life. No other Christian community has given so much attention to all the details and dynamics of the spiritual life or has fostered such a range of devotional practices. No other Christian community has made so much of formal religious communities or encouraged them and multiplied them as spiritual resources to such a degree.

The Catholic Church has always held those who are deeply devoted to prayer and contemplation in high regard and has formally declared some of these "contemplatives" to be saints.

There is, therefore, a commitment to spirituality and community in the Catholic Church which makes it unique.

Comprehensiveness

There has been no Christian Church which has been as universal and diverse as the Catholic Church. This comprehensiveness is suggested by the very word "catholic." It has absorbed more cultural influence and lived through more centuries as a unified body of believers than any other Christian community. It allows dissent and censures it. It is changing continually and yet somehow seems to be

immobile. Its universality is rooted in local communities which are, paradoxically, authenticated through a global and distant network of structures.

It is no easy task to isolate distinctive elements in the Catholic Church. One needs to do this in a way that shows differences but yet does not disparage other Christian communities. It is necessary to celebrate the greatness of Catholicism and yet not become triumphalistic or unaware of the failures of the Church and of its need for humility.

It is imperative to affirm Catholicism so that it is truly distinguished from other Churches, and yet not to lose sight of the fact that the elements the Christian Churches have in common are more impressive than the features which divide them.

All Christian communities make significant reference to the basic elements of the Church. All of them believe in Christ as Lord and Savior, pray for the Spirit and celebrate Liturgy and Scripture.

Thus, we Catholics and other Christians know that one day we shall be a unified body of believers, expressing in our ecclesial life the oneness Christ has already made present in our hearts.

(photo left) All the essential features of the Church's life reach us in a community whose members we know and whose pastoral leaders know us.

10

FIDELITY AND DESTINY

No one can look at the history and life of the Catholic Church with an unbiased attitude and fail to marvel at all it has accomplished.

It may not be too much to suggest that in terms of numbers and influence on the world, in terms of durability and contributions to human development, no other institution has been so successful.

The Catholic Church has kept alive the memory of Christ and written the Gospel. It has broken bread in the name of Jesus and

Christianity is always at its best when it is reduced to human proportions.

conserved the Spirit and Tradition of his life. It has baptized and consoled the dying, enabled people to believe their sins were forgiven, and proclaimed marriage as a sacrament. Through its ministers and preachers, it has encircled the globe and spoken in all the languages the world speaks.

It has commissioned popes and hermits, cardinals and monks, bishops and nuns, priests and laity, married couples and celibates, leaders of nations and contemplatives to speak in its name and to teach the message of Christ.

The Catholic Church has canonized saints for centuries and developed spiritual theologies. It has taught people to pray and settled their anxieties. It has created a wide range of devotional practices and led people on pilgrimages of repentance. It has made the Christian lives of people

a prime object of its attention. It has organized parish and diocesan life into communities where Christ is made accessible to people who believe in him.

A Human Church

The Church has not done all of this without its own record of shameful deeds. There have been things done in its name, officially and otherwise, which have wounded people and obstructed the mission of Christ.

The Church has been a Church of sinners, even on the highest levels of its institutional life. And yet, somehow it has never lost its original vision nor denied its original constitution. It has never ceased preaching the very Gospel which has brought it back to the Christ from whom it may have wandered. It has been faithful, in the

deepest recesses of its being, to the Christ whom it has never fully forsaken and whom it has loved with all its heart, at its best moments and in its best members.

The Church has no right to be vain or complacent about its success. Its record has not been perfect. For all its splendor, the Church is not about the Church, any more than a marriage is about a marriage.

The point of a marriage is something other than the marriage, namely, the relationship of the couple, a relationship of which marriage is a sign or sacrament. It is not as though the couple are committed to the marriage; they are committed to each other in the marriage.

The Church, quite simply, is about Christ and about the relationship people have with Christ. The Church is a sign or sacrament of that relationship in community and of that Christ who is the center of its life.

And so if the Church has prevailed, it has done so not because it kept alive its own memory or broke Bread in its own name. The Tradition and Scripture of the Church have come to it from more than its human resources and have been inspired by the Spirit that Christ promised to it. The Church is compelling because the Christ it preaches captivates people.

When the Church celebrates all its sacraments and summons its authority legitimately, when it develops ministries to deepen Christian life, it does all this in Christ. Take away Jesus and the Church becomes an empty shell.

When people are deeply moved by the Church, it is the parables and the Christmas story, the Passion and the Passover supper, the washing of the feet and the agonizing death on the

cross, the Easter sunrise and the flaming glory of the Holy Spirit which moves them. If the Church succeeds, it owes all this to its Master and Savior.

Nor should the Church become enamored of its past. The Church is not a museum but a pilgrim people. In many ways, it seems that its mission has just begun. It is seeking now to become a world Church, even more liberated from its European and Western cultural conditioning. It fashions its hope, as it has never done before, in terms of global peace and

"For God and before God, the human being is always unique and unrepeatable, somebody thought of and chosen from eternity, someone called and identified by his or her own name" (John Paul II).

All ministry, then, lay and ordained comes from the community... from its shared Baptism, from its common priesthood.

international justice, in terms of women as well as men, in terms of laity as well as clergy, in terms of all believers from all religious traditions, and even from those which profess no formal faith but are filled with good will.

At the end of the second millennium of its life, the Church celebrated the Second Vatican Council which has become a summary of all that was best in the Catholic Church of the past and a summons to a comprehensiveness and catholicity more expansive than anything the Church has yet experienced.

If all this be true, then the Church is truly worth our fidelity to it.

One of the most urgent questions of our day concerns the freedom of the individual in relation to massive social and religious institutions. In a sense, it is a question that has always been with us, a question that will never be fully resolved. Even on the most basic level of institutional life, namely the family, the tension between personal freedom and community loyalty is not settled. Spouses with each other and children with parents endlessly seek to balance autonomy and commitment.

As the challenge of individual charisms and institutional claims reaches us, it emerges as an old, permanent and urgent concern. If it ceases to be raised, that will be a sign that institutions have crushed all individual identity or that individualism has dissolved all institutional bonding. It is, therefore, necessary that the issue be kept alive and creatively addressed.

In our freedom as individual persons or in our autonomy as small communities of believers, it is wise to keep in mind the limits of our resources. The capacity to accomplish global objectives for the sake of Christ is begun in each of our lives but is not completed there. Jesus washed the feet of each of his disciples at the Last Supper and invited them to receive bread and wine one by one. But he also asked them to preach the Gospel to the ends of the earth and to wait for him through all future time. Even in its initial faith in the Risen Christ, the Church was committed to a mission which went beyond all its resources.

It is worth recalling that the freedom each of us expresses individually and in small communities is a circumscribed freedom, often limited in its scope. In our own lives and in those of our immediate friends and neighbors, we tend to define ourselves by one race or even one gender, one moment of time or one socio-economic group. We tend to limit the influence of the whole range of history and of the wide spectrum of the world.

The twentieth century has been the most creative in history in its effort to form a global community of nations. This has been the century of the League of Nations, of the United Nations, of a World Court and a World Bank, of global communications systems and a world monetary network. This has been the century when a World Health Organization, a Food and Agricultural Organization, Unicef and a High Commissioner for Refugees have struggled to deal with problems on an international level.

We know that these efforts have not always been successful, but there has never been anything like them before in history. They testify, by their very creation, to our inadequacy in solving problems on a national level alone. Questions of the environment and the seas, economics and food, health and disarmament, travel and communication can no longer be addressed intelligently as national problems.

The Church tells us that without love we perish as a species and that there is a power in all of us which prevails in the darkness and brings light to a grateful world. No political or economic leader can tell us this as credibly as can the Church.

When the Church acts from its deepest life, it convinces men and women that there is something sacred about life and that the world is a place where grace happens and where God dwells.

A Church of Promise

There is a movement and force in the world community toward greater and greater relatedness. Just as once, nation states ended tribal conflicts in their own boundaries by bringing smaller groups into national groupings, so now national ''tribes'' in the boundaries of this planet are tending toward global unity and consciousness.

On the religious scene, this has been the century of ecumenism and interreligious dialogue. Prayer and worship, theology and peace, justice and contemplation cross the planet, and become the means by which each community of believers seeks to enrich other communities of believers.

Buddhism and Christianity, Hinduism, Judaism and Islam are sources of inspiration and resources of human enrichment. This global sense of religious faith does not lead to indifferentism but to an awareness of the diversity of ways in which human beings have sought God.

So, it is no coincidence that the founding of the United Nations and Vatican Council II occurred within less than twenty years of each other.

In both of these events, the yearning for global unity and harmony were made manifest.

Human harmony will not be achieved by political and economic means alone even though these elements are necessary pieces of the puzzle.

At some point in this forward movement, issues of conscience and ethics, of transcendence and meaning must be addressed. There must be global religious institutions to remind the human family of the mystery and majesty of the human heart, of the greatness but insufficiency of human potential, of the peace that only faith brings and of the life that love engenders. It is here that Catholicism may have an utterly unique and irreplaceable role to play. The papacy, for example, has the capacity to address the United Nations and the world at large and make an impact that no other religious office has. This is a resource for the human family which must be valued and utilized.

It may well be that of all the religious communities in the world, none has used ritual and symbol, sacrament and liturgy more creatively or extensively than the Catholic Church. The Church, then, may possess the potential to create from its resources and life the rituals a world community needs for its unity.

There has been no other religious institution which has become inculturated in so many nations and peoples as has Catholicism. This too may give it the capacity to express the world's unity in a way all the human family can call its own.

Fidelity to the Church is a means to the deeper fidelities to Christ and to all humanity. The Church may well be the most effective way we can reach Christ and the world. In its best Tradition, it is for everyone. In its proclamation of Christ and Scripture, it reminds us that there has been only one creation and that there is only one destiny for all of us. In its ministry and spiritual theology, it recalls to us our brokenness and our need for healing. It is not only our bodies and our world but our hearts and spirits which must be renewed and refreshed.

The Church addresses the whole human family and invites us to contemplation, asking us to cease at times from all our labors and anxieties and to know that we did not create ourselves and that we cannot prolong our lives forever.

The Church tells us that without love we perish as a species and that there is a power in all of us which prevails in the darkness and brings light to a grateful world. No political or economic leader can tell us this as credibly as can the Church.

When the Church acts from its deepest life, it convinces men and women that there is something sacred about life and that the world is a place where grace happens and where God dwells.

The Church, therefore, is still young. Its journey through time has hardly begun. We who believe in the Church are faithful to our own destiny by being faithful to the Church. At some profound level of the Church's life, Christ and the Spirit are present. In the heart and core of the Church, we encounter also ourselves and the world, the human family and its invincible future.

"Christ was sent by the Father 'to bring good news to the poor...to heal the contrite of heart' (*Luke* 4:18), 'to seek and to save what was lost' (*Luke* 19:10). Similarly, the Church encompasses with love all those who are afflicted by human misery, and the Church recognizes in those who are poor and who suffer, the image of our poor and suffering founder. The Church does all in its power to relieve their need and in them it strives to serve Christ.

"...By the power of the risen Lord the Church is given strength to overcome, in patience and love, all sorrows and difficulties...so that the Church may reveal in the world faithfully, however darkly, the mystery of the Lord...."

adapted from
Vatican Council II 1964
DOGMATIC CONSTITUTION ON THE CHURCH *IV:32*

POPES OF THE CATHOLIC CHURCH

The history of the Popes reflects the turbulent ages in which many of them lived. Precise details about their dates, titles, and the spelling of their names are not always available. The legitimate succession of some in times of war and schism is questioned. The following list provides the name, nationality, and date of death or abdication of those officially recognized by the Catholic Church today in accordance with the latest scholarship. The reference to their nationality approximates present national/regional boundaries.

1. St. Peter (*Jewish*), 67.
2. St. Linus (*Italian*), 76.
3. St. Anacletus (*Italian*), 88.
4. St. Clement I (*Italian*), 97.
5. St. Evaristus (*Greek*), 105.
6. St. Alexander I (*Italian*), 115.
7. St. Sixtus I (*Italian*), 125.
8. St. Telesphorus (*Greek*), 136.
9. St. Hyginus (*Greek*), 140.
10. St. Pius I (*Italian*), 155.
11. St. Anicetus (*Syrian*), 166.
12. St. Soter (*Italian*), 175.
13. St. Eleutherius (*Greek*), 189.
14. St. Victor I (*African*), 199.
15. St. Zephyrinus (*Italian*), 217.
16. St. Callistus I (*Italian*), 222.
17. St. Urban I (*Italian*), 230.
18. St. Pontian (*Italian*), 235.
19. St. Anterus (*Greek*), 236.
20. St. Fabian (*Italian*), 250.
21. St. Cornelius (*Italian*), 253.
22. St. Lucius I (*Italian*), 254.
23. St. Stephen I (*Italian*), 257.
24. St. Sixtus II (*Greek*), 258.
25. St. Dionysius (*Greek?*), 268.
26. St. Felix I (*Italian*), 274.
27. St. Eutychian (*Italian*), 283.
28. St. Gaius (*Italian*),296.
29. St. Marcellinus (*Italian*), 304.
30. St. Marcellus I (*Italian*), 309.
31. St. Eusebius (*Greek*), 309.
32. St. Miltiades (*African*), 314.
33. St. Sylvester I (*Italian*), 335.
34. St. Mark (*Italian*), 336.
35. St. Julius I (*Italian*), 352.
36. Liberius (*Italian*), 366.
37. St. Damasus I (*Spanish*), 384.
38. St. Siricius (*Italian*), 399.
39. St. Anastasius I (*Italian*), 401.
40. St. Innocent I (*Italian*), 417.
41. St. Zozimus (*Greek*), 418.
42. St. Boniface I (*Italian*), 422.
43. St. Celestine I (*Italian*), 432.
44. St. Sixtus III (*Italian*), 440.
45. St. Leo I (*Italian*), 461.
46. St. Hilary (*Italian*), 468.
47. St. Simplicius (*Italian*), 483.
48. St. Felix III, (*Italian*), 492.
49. St. Gelasius I (*African*), 496.
50. Anastasius II (*Italian*), 498.
51. St. Symmachus (*Italian*), 514.
52. St. Hormisdas (*Italian*), 523.
53. St. John I (*Italian*), 526.
54. St. Felix IV (*Italian*), 530.
55. Boniface II (*Italian*), 532.
56. John II (*Italian*), 535.
57. St. Agapitus I (*Italian*), 536.
58. St. Silverius (*Italian*), 537.
59. Vigilius (*Italian*), 555.
60. Pelagius I (*Italian*), 561.
61. John III (*Italian*), 574.
62. Benedict I (*Italian*), 579.
63. Pelagius II (*Italian*), 590.
64. St. Gregory I (*Italian*), 604.
65. Sabinian (*Italian*), 606.
66. Boniface III (*Italian*), 607.
67. St. Boniface IV (*Italian*), 615.
68. St. Deusdedit [Adeodatus I] (*Italian*), 618.
69. Boniface V (*Italian*), 625.
70. Honorius I (*Italian*), 638.
71. Severinus (*Italian*), 640.
72. John IV (*Italian*), 642.
73. Theodore I (*Greek*), 649.
74. St. Martin I (*Italian*), 655.
75. St. Eugene I (*Italian*), 657.
76. St. Vitalian (*Italian*), 672.
77. Adeodatus II (*Italian*), 676.
78. Donus (*Italian*), 678.
79. St. Agatho (*Italian*), 681.
80. St. Leo II (*Italian*), 683.
81. St. Benedict II (*Italian*), 685.
82. John V (*Syrian*), 686.
83. Conon (*unknown*), 687.
84. St. Sergius I (*Syrian*), 701.
85. John VI (*Greek*), 705.
86. John VII (*Greek*), 707.
87. Sisinnius (*Syrian*), 708.
88. Constantine (*Syrian*), 715.
89. St. Gregory II (*Italian*),731.
90. St. Gregory III (*Syrian*), 741.
91. St. Zachary (*Greek*), 752.
92. Stephen II (III) (*Italian*), 757.
93. St. Paul I (*Italian*), 767.
94. Stephen III (*Italian*), 772.
95. Adrian I (*Italian*), 795.
96. St. Leo III (*Italian*), 816.
97. Stephen IV (*Italian*), 817.
98. St. Paschal I (*Italian*), 824.
99. Eugene II (*Italian*), 827.
100. Valentine (*Italian*), 827.
101. Gregory IV (*Italian*), 844.
102. Sergius II (*Italian*), 847.
103. St. Leo IV (*Italian*), 855.
104. Benedict III (*Italian*), 858.
105. St. Nicholas I (*Italian*), 867.
106. Adrian II (*Italian*),872.
107. John VIII (*Italian*), 882.
108. Marinus I (*Italian*), 884.
109. St. Adrian III (*Italian*), 885.
110. Stephen V (*Italian*), 891.
111. Formosus (*Italian*), 896.
112. Boniface VI (*Italian*), 896.
113. Stephen VI (*Italian*), 897.
114. Romanus (*Italian*), 897.
115. Theodore II (*Italian*), 897.
116. John IX (*Italian*), 900.
117. Benedict IV (*Italian*),903.
118. Leo V (*Italian*), 903.
119. Sergius III (*Italian*), 911.
120. Anastasius III (*Italian*),913.
121. Lando (*Italian*), 914.
122. John X (*Italian*), 928.
123. Leo VI (*Italian*), 928.
124. Stephen VII (*Italian*), 931.
125. John XI (*Italian*),935.
126. Leo VII (*Italian*), 939.
127. Stephen VIII (*Italian*), 942.
128. Marinus II (*Italian*), 946.
129. Agapetus II (*Italian*), 955.
130. John XII (*Italian*), 964.
131. Leo VIII (*Italian*), 965.
132. Benedict V (*Italian*), 966.
133. John XIII (*Italian*), 972.
134. Benedict VI (*Italian*), 974.
135. Benedict VII (*Italian*), 983.
136. John XIV (*Italian*), 984.
137. John XV (*Italian*), 996.
138. Gregory V (*Italian*), 999.

139. Sylvester II (*French*), 1003.
140. John XVII (*Italian*), 1003.
141. John XVIII (*Italian*), 1009.
142. Sergius IV (*Italian*), 1012.
143. Benedict VIII (*Italian*), 1024.
144. John XIX (*Italian*), 1032.
145. Benedict IX (*Italian*),
    1044 (***deposed***).
146. Sylvester III (*Italian*), 1045.
147. Benedict IX, (2nd reign),
    1045 (***abdicated***).
148. Gregory VI (*Italian*), 1046.
149. Clement II (*German*), 1047.
150. Benedict IX (3rd reign),
    1048 (***deposed***).
151. Damasus II (*German*), 1048.
152. St. Leo IX (*German*), 1054.
153. Victor II (*German*), 1057.
154. Stephen IX (*French*), 1058.
155. Nicholas II (*French*), 1061.
156. Alexander II (*Italian*), 1073.
157. St. Gregory VII (*Italian*),1085.
158. Blessed Victor III
    (*Italian*), 1087.
159. Blessed Urban II
    (*French*), 1099.
160. Paschal II (*Italian*), 1118.
161. Gelasius II (*Italian*), 1119.
162. Callistus II (*French*), 1124.
163. Honorius II (*Italian*), 1130.
164. Innocent II (*Italian*), 1143.
165. Celestine II (*Italian*), 1144.
166. Lucius II (*Italian*), 1145.
167. Blessed Eugene III
    (*Italian*), 1153.
168. Anastasius IV (*Italian*), 1154.
169. Adrian IV (*English*), 1159.
170. Alexander III (*Italian*), 1181.
171. Lucius III (*Italian*), 1185.
172. Urban III (*Italian*), 1187.
173. Gregory VII (*Italian*), 1187.
174. Clement III (*Italian*), 1191.
175. Celestine III (*Italian*), 1198.
176. Innocent III (*Italian*), 1216.
177. Honorius III (*Italian*), 1227.
178. Gregory IX (*Italian*), 1241.
179. Celestine IV (*Italian*), 1241.
180. Innocent IV (*Italian*), 1254.
181. Alexander IV (*Italain*), 1261.
182. Urban IV (*French*), 1264.
183. Clement IV (*French*), 1268.
184. Blessed Gregory X
    (*Italian*), 1276.

185. Blessed Innocent V
    (*French*), 1276.
186. Adrian V (*Italian*), 1276.
187. John XXI (*Portuguese*), 1277.
188. Nicholas III (*Italian*),1280.
189. Martin IV (*French*), 1285.
190. Honorius IV (*Italian*), 1287.
191. Nicholas IV (*Italian*), 1292.
192. St. Celestine V (*Italian*),
    1294 (***abdicated***).
193. Boniface VIII (*Italian*), 1303.
194. Blessed Benedict XI
    (*Italian*), 1304.
195. Clement V (*French*), 1314.
196. John XXII (*French*), 1334.
197. Benedict XII (*French*), 1342.
198. Clement VI (*French*), 1352.
199. Innocent VI (*French*), 1362.
200. Blessed Urban V (*French*),
    1370.
201. Gregory XI (*French*), 1378.
202. Urban VI (*Italian*), 1389.
203. Boniface IX (*Italian*), 1404.
204. Innocent VII (*Italian*), 1406.
205. Gregory XII (*Italian*),
    1415 (***abdicated***).
206. Martin V (*Italian*), 1431.
207. Eugene IV (*Italian*), 1447.
208. Nicholas V (*Italian*), 1455.
209. Callistus III (*Spanish*), 1458.
210. Pius II (*Italian*), 1464.
211. Paul II (*Italian*), 1471.
212. Sixtus IV (*Italian*), 1484.
213. Innocent VIII (*Italian*), 1492.
214. Alexander VI (*Spanish*), 1503.
215. Pius III (*Italian*), 1503.
216. Julius II (*Italian*), 1513.
217. Leo X (*Italian*), 1521.
218. Adrian VI (*Dutch*), 1523.
219. Clement VII (*Italian*), 1534.
220. Paul III (*Italian*), 1549.
221. Julius III (*Italian*), 1555.
222. Marcellus II (*Italian*), 1555.
223. Paul IV (*Italian*), 1559.
224. Pius IV (*Italian*), 1565.
225. St. Pius V (*Italian*), 1572.
226. Gregory XIII (*Italian*),1585.
227. Sixtus V (*Italian*), 1590.
228. Urban VII (*Italian*), 1590.
229. Gregory XIV (*Italian*), 1591.
230. Innocent IX (*Italian*), 1591.
231. Clement VIII (*Italian*), 1605.
232. Leo XI (*Italian*), 1605.

233. Paul V (*Italian*), 1621.
234. Gregory XV (*Italian*), 1623.
235. Urban VIII (*Italian*), 1644.
236. Innocent X (*Italian*), 1655.
237. Alexander VII (*Italian*), 1667.
238. Clement IX (*Italian*), 1669.
239. Clement X (*Italian*), 1676.
240. Blessed Innocent XI
    (*Italian*), 1689.
241. Alexander VIII (*Italian*), 1691.
242. Innocent XII (*Italian*), 1700.
243. Clement XI (*Italian*), 1721.
244. Innocent XIII (*Italian*), 1724.
245. Benedict XIII (*Italian*), 1730.
246. Clement XII (*Italian*), 1740.
147. Benedict XIV (*Italian*), 1758.
248. Clement XIII (*Italian*), 1769.
249. Clement XIV (*Italian*), 1774.
250. Pius VI (*Italian*), 1799.
251. Pius VII (*Italian*), 1823.
252. Leo XII (*Italian*), 1829.
253. Pius VIII (*Italian*), 1830.
254. Gregory XVI (*Italian*), 1846.
255. Pius IX (*Italian*), 1878.
256. Leo XIII (*Italian*), 1903.
257. St. Pius X (*Italian*), 1914.
258. Benedict XV (*Italian*), 1922.
259. Pius XI (*Italian*), 1939.
260. Pius XII (*Italian*), 1958.
261. John XXIII (*Italian*), 1963.
262. Paul VI (*Italian*), 1978.
263. John Paul I (*Italian*), 1978.
264. John Paul II (*Polish*).

POPES BY NATIONALITY:

Italian: 213
French: 16
Greek: 13
Syrian: 6
German: 4
African: 3
Spanish: 3
Jewish: 1
English: 1
Portuguese: 1
Dutch: 1
Polish: 1
Unknown: 1

AVERAGE REIGN OF POPES:

Seven years, four months

Glossary

(Numbers following each entry refer to pages in the text.)

BODY OF CHRIST:
After Jesus' resurrection, his followers used a single term, "the Body of Christ," to express three distinct realities: the risen body of Christ, the Eucharist, and the Church. They indicated that all three meanings had one thing in common: the presence of Christ. He had appeared to the the disciples alive again, although his physical body had been transformed. That experience helped them also to recognize Jesus' abiding presence under the appearance of bread and wine as he had told them at the Last Supper. That, too, was his transformed Body. And finally, they discovered that their own vocation was to become transformed people, the Church, the Body of Christ, with the risen Christ as their Head *(cf. pp. 21-24)*.

BASIC CHRISTIAN COMMUNITIES:
Millions of Catholics in search of an adult understanding and living experience of their faith have returned to the New Testament practice of gathering in small groups as "House Churches." These stable communities of mutual support guide their members to a personal experience of God in a non-threatening setting of dialogue centered on sacred Scripture and daily life. The development of the gifts or charisms of each member contributes to a network of services extending to the wider parish community through which they are linked to the universal Church *(cf. Chapter Eight)*.

THE BREAKING OF THE BREAD:
When Jesus ceremonially "broke bread" at the Last Supper (Matthew 22:26-28; Luke 22:26-28), his gesture contained many meanings:

the sharing of food, the sacrificial breaking of his body that would soon take place on the cross, and the sign of the new covenant with God -- and with one another. After the resurrection, Jesus' followers recognized this ceremony as the symbol, goal and source of their common life as the new people of God. Breaking bread as sisters and brothers at the same table with Christ inspired the first Christians to adopt a distinctive lifestyle in community *(Acts 2:42-47)* for which the "Breaking of the Bread" became a living symbol and task *(cf. pp. 21-24)*.

COLLEGIALITY:
The II Vatican Council modified the age old centralization of teaching authority in the Pope by restoring a more biblical image. Peter and the other apostles formed an apostolic "college" of shared responsibility in the service of God's people. Their successors, the bishops acting in unity with the Pope, do the same. This shared responsibility becomes most evident at an ecumenical council whose head is always the Pope, and to a lesser degree in the bishops' synods which the Pope calls every three years to consult with the bishops to help him in governing the Church. Today, most bishops extend this collaboration procedure by calling upon all priests and laity to cooperate in proclaiming the Gospel and in nourishing the Church *(cf. pp. 71, 82-83, 105, 109)*.

ECUMENISM:
The word, *ecumenism*, means "the whole wide world." An ecumenical council represents the local Churches of the Catholic world under the leadership of the Pope. In a wider sense, *ecumenism* refers to a movement to reunite all Christian Churches *(cf. p. 109)*.

INFALLIBILITY:
The Church's mission is to promote

God's Reign under the guidance of the Holy Spirit. The protection needed not to fall away essentially in pursuing that task is called *indefectibility*. The positive guidance of the Spirit to teach God's message "immune from error" is known as *infalllibility,* which may be said about the Church as a whole or about the Pope as its leader. Immunity from error in teaching resides first of all in the whole people of God, and that teaching authority is exercised collegially. Infallibility also applies to the Pope in a very restricted sense, that is, only when he intends to define solemnly and infallibly some matter of faith or morals. That must take place always in unity with the whole Church, and happens seldom in history. Vatican II depicted the Church as a "pilgrim people," growing in its understanding of the Good News and in striving to fulfil its demands. Therefore, even solemnly defined teachings can be expanded at later times as more insights are gained and modern needs require *(cf. pp. 75, 109)*.

MAGISTERIUM:
The "teaching authority" of the Church in clarifying Scripture and Tradition is called *magisterium*. Strictly speaking, it refers to the power entrusted by Christ to the Pope and bishops to define and interpret the contents and the practice of the Christian faith. In recent years, bishops' conferences have exercised this office in a more consultative manner, asking the advice of both clergy and laity, thereby recognizing the teaching authority of the whole people of God who share through Baptism in the priestly, prophetic and kingly office of Christ *(cf. p. 109)*.

MINISTRY AND CHRISTIAN SERVICE:
The Church is a community of believers called to service or priest-

hood as a "priestly people."
Besides this common priesthood,
there is a ministerial priesthood
made up of ordained ministers
officially invested with special and
permanent powers to nourish and
guide the Christian community in
unity and love. This ministry applies
especially to proclaiming the Gospel
and administering the sacraments.
Today ordained ministers are
delegating some functions to the
laity, for example, to act as lectors,
to distribute Communion, to instruct
others in the faith, and to visit the
sick. Some refer to this activity by
the laity as "ministries," others
prefer the term, "Christian services"
(*Constitution on the Church*, #10,
33, 35) (*cf. pp. 82-87*).

SYNOPTIC GOSPELS:

The Gospels according to Matthew,
Mark and Luke are called the "Synoptics" (Greek = *see side by side*),
because of their many similarities.
Matthew and Luke are said to have
borrowed many things from Mark's
Gospel as well as from other
sources. The resulting parallels
become evident when the three Gospels are compared side by side (*cf. p.
24*).

TRADITION:

A theme permeating the entire Bible
is that God remains actively present
within the community of believers.
In their hymns, poetry, processions,
worship and creeds, the faithful
expressed their gratitude for God's
continued guidance and care. The
totality of Christian existence
became a record of their experience,
and that testimony today is known as
"Tradition." In order to preserve
that witness for later generations, the
faithful began writing down their
stories and formalizing their annual
religious celebrations of them. This
written record became "sacred
Scripture" which was finalized
within a few generations after Jesus'

resurrection. In contrast, the community reflection process continues.
Therefore, Catholics base their faith
on both the written testimony of
Scripture and on the living Tradition
of the Church which together form a
united, consistent process of revelation (*cf. pp. 36-39*).

VATICAN II:
DOCUMENTS OF THE
SECOND VATICAN COUNCIL:

The twenty-first ecumenical council,
Vatican II (1962-65), produced 16
official documents. These serve the
multiple purpose of reviving the
Church's self-image rooted in sacred
Scripture, of defining a vision of re
form unparalleled in modern history,
and of clarifying the Church's relationship and responsibility toward
the rest of humanity. The documents most frequently referred to in
the Catholic Home Library Series
are those referring to *Divine Revelation, The Church, The Church in the
Modern World,* and *The Sacred
Liturgy.*

Index

Adam and Eve 11
alternative churches 105
alternative communities 35
Anointing 62, 63, 71, 72, 74, 106
assembly 71, 80, 104
authority 23, 67, 68, 69, 72, 91, 107-9
autonomy 116-7
Baptism 13, 14, 38, 59-80, 62, 63, 80-3
belief 25, 73
behavior 73
bishops 74-5, 108
Body of Christ 16, 21, 23, 27, 62, 80, 86
Breaking of Bread 21, 23, 69, 71, 107
Catholicism 103-5, 111, 119
Christ 25, 26, 43, 45-6, 49, 57, 64, 91,93
Christmas 13, 17, 91, 106, 115
Church 11, 13
   assembly 71, 80, 104, 108
   authority 71, 72, 91, 107-9
   calling 65
   central focus 97
   change 33, 55, 56, 57, 58
   contemplative love 97
   continuity 33
   decisions 31, 33, 36, 38, 56, 72-4, 91
   Easter 47, 56
   failures 111
   family model 11, 13, 15, 23, 24, 65,
      68, 69, 71
   fidelity 116, 119
   growth and change 30, 56, 57, 71
   heart of 26-7
   humanity of 114, 119
   institution 24
   longevity 35
   love 63
   marriage 106, 115
   meditation 93
   memory 49, 57
   ministry 82, 85, 86, 109, 119
   mission 117
   nature of 63, 107
   parish 89, 90, 92-3
   sacramentality 106-7
   sacraments 65
   sins of 104
   spiritual life 111
   spouse of Christ 13
   universal 89, 90, 111
Church in the Modern World 107
collegial principle 39, 83, 105
commitment 116
Community
   alternative 35
   assembly 71, 80, 104
   authority 69, 72, 107
   Church 17, 21, 23, 27, 42, 90, 92
   contemplative love 94, 96, 97
   Eucharistic gathering 26

faith 43
family 69, 90
formation 96
Liturgy 46
love 63
marriage 106
ministry 82, 92, 109
mission 92
nature of 45
past and future 46,114-6
People of God 79
Sacramentality 106-7
Second Vatican Council 80
spiritual life 111
parish 89, 90, 92-3
universal 96
universal Church 90
Confirmation 60, 62, 63
conscience 67, 68, 72, 91
contemplation 17, 93
continuity 33
Creation 10, 11, 13
Cross 16
decisions 31, 33, 36, 38, 56, 72-4, 91
Easter 17, 20, 21
   Christ 24-25, 27
   Church 47, 56
   Eucharist 26
ecumenical councils 29, 39, 75, 108
ecumenism 105, 118
equality 23
Eucharist 24, 26, 63, 80
   Church 47, 56
   and the Gospels 24
   Easter 26
   pivotal sacrament 59, 62
   marriage 64
Exodus 15
faith 25
fidelity 116, 119
freedom 117
Genesis 10
global unity 118-119
history 72, 113
infallibility 35, 109
institution 24, 69, 116
Jesus 11, 13
   center 13, 15
   Church 13-4, 39, 56
   Cross of 16
   Easter 17, 24
   life span 19-20
   Presence 57
   reformer 15
   Scripture 43
John the Baptist 13, 14
Last Judgment 71
law 15-6, 71
life 113

Liturgy 46, 47, 49, 56, 64
Love
   contemplative 93, 94, 96-7
   and the Cross 16
   enemies 71
   heart of the Church 87
   human misery 121
   knowledge 45-6
   law 15, 71
   power 119
   marital 11
   works of 107
Lumen Gentium 79
man 10-11, 13, 16, 17
magisterium 109
meditation 17, 93
memory 20-3, 43-9, 65, 69, 71, 85, 107
ministry 23, 82, 85-7, 91, 109
mission 92, 117
marital love 11, 64
marriage 63, 64, 65, 91, 106
Mary 11, 13, 16, 38
New Testament 27
obedience 14, 108
office-holder 15, 74
optimism 109
order 73
Orders 63, 64, 106
ordained minister 64
Orthodox 104-5
papacy 39, 75, 90, 105, 108-9, 119
parish council 83, 91, 96
parish 89-90, 92-93
Pentecost 23, 38, 83
People of God 79
Peter 38, 39, 74, 75
priesthood 82, 91
Protestant 104-5
Reconciliation 62, 63, 106
Reign of God 107
sacramentality 106-7
sacraments 38, 58, 63, 65, 85, 90
Scripture 36, 38, 41-2, 45, 46, 47, 49,
   56, 69, 71, 72, 92, 105, 107, 119
Second Coming 49
Second Vatican Council 64, 77-9, 80,
   82, 104, 105, 116, 118
social justice 94, 96, 107
Spirit 21, 23, 26-7, 33, 35-9, 56, 60, 64,
   71, 80, 91, 92, 94, 109
spiritual life 111
symbols 59
synoptics 24
Tradition 35, 36, 39, 42-3, 46-7, 49, 56,
   64, 69, 71, 92, 105, 107, 119
vocation 14
Word of God 14, 94
woman 10-11, 13, 16, 17, 71
worship 46

Photo Credits

Cover Photo: Bob Kuhn
6: Anthony Boccaccio
8-9: FC (Michael McBlane)
10, 11: American Stock Photography
11: American Stock Photography
12: Anthony Boccaccio
13: Catherine Busch
14: FC (Michael McBlane)
15: Edd Anthony, OFM
16: Anthony Boccaccio
17: Edd Anthony, OFM
18-19: Anthony Boccaccio
20: Bill Barrett
21: Maryknoll Missioners - Eric Wheater
22: FC (Alan Oddie)
23: Bill Barrett
24: Franciscan Communications
25: Maryknoll Missioners - Eric Wheater
26: Bill Barrett
27: FC (Michael McBlane)
28-29: Dienst
30: FC (Michael McBlane)
31: Anthony Boccaccio
32: Karl Holtsnider
33: Linda Rowley
34, 35: FC (Michael McBlane)
36: Maryknoll Missioners - Eric Wheater
37: FC (Michael McBlane)
38, 39: Bill Barrett
40-41: FC (Catherine Busch)
42: The Cleveland Museum of Art--Gift of Hanna Fund
   50.399
43: FC (Michael McBlane)
44: FC (Michael McBlane)
45: FC (Michael McBlane)
46: American Stock Photography
47: FC (Catherine Busch)
48: Dienst
49: FC (Jack Quinn, SJ)
50-51: clockwise from upper left:
   a+b) Eric Wheater;
   c) FC;
   d) FC (Michael McBlane);
   e+f) FC;
   g) FC (Alan Oddie);
52: Anthony Boccaccio
54-55: Catholic Relief Services
56: FC (Michael McBlane)
57: Bill Barrett
58: FC (Neil Sapienza)
59: FC (Anthony Boccaccio)
60: Maryknoll Missioners (E.J. Hahn)
61: Bill Barrett
62: FC (Neil Sapienza)
63, 64: Franciscan Communications
65: Bill Barrett
66-67: FC (Jack Quinn, SJ)
68: FC (Jack Quinn, SJ)
69: Anthony Boccaccio

70: Franciscan Communications
71: Dienst
72: FC (Neil Sapienza)
73: FC (Catherine Busch)
74: Dienst
75: FC
76-77: FC (Michael McBlane)
78: Franciscan Communications
79: Anthony boccaccio
80: Maryknoll Missioners - D.J. Casey
81: FC (Michael McBlane)
82: FC (Catherine Busch)
83: Catholic Relief Service - Silverman
84, 85: Catholic Relief Service
86: FC (Michael McBlane)
87: Anthony Boccaccio
88-89: Edd Anthony, OFM
90, 91: FC (Michael McBlane)
92: Franciscan Communications
93 above: FC (Michael McBlane);
93 below: Edd Anthony, OFM
94, 95: Anthony Boccaccio
96: Maryknoll Missioners - Eric Wheater
97: Franciscan Communications
98-99: clockwise from upper left:
   a) FC (Catherine Busch);
   b+c) FC;
   d) FC (Michael McBlane);
   e) FC (Catherine Busch);
   f) FC;
   g) FC (Michael McBlane);
   h) FC (Catherine Busch)
100: American Stock Photography
102-103: Anthony Boccaccio
104: David Duncan
105, 106: FC (Michael McBlane)
107: Dienst
108: FC (Michael McBlane)
109: FC (Catherine Busch)
110: Maryknoll Missioners - Eric Wheater
112-113: American Stock Photography
114: Edd Anthony, OFM
115, 116: Eric Wheater
117: United Nations
118: FC (Michael McBlane)
120-121: clockwise from upper left:
   a) Catholic Relief Services;
   b) United Nations;
   c) Anthony Boccaccio;
   d) United Nations;
   e+f) FC (Michael McBlane)
   g) FC;
   h) Dienst;
   i) FC

AUTHOR: Anthony Padovano, PhD, STD is a
Catholic theologian and minister. He has doctorates both
in literature and theology. He lectures as professor of
American Literature and Religious Studies at Ramapo
College of New Jersey, and as adjunct full professor
of Theology at Fordham University of New York. Dr.
Padovano has written national pastoral letters for the
American Catholic Bishops and is author of twenty
books. He has won awards for three of his plays, and he
lectures world-wide on theological and spiritual topics.
Dr. Padovano has given extensive interviews on major
television networks in the United States and in Europe.
He was founding president of the Diocese of Paterson's
Justice and Peace Commission.

Franciscan Communications, a non-profit organization,
seeks to communicate the gospel vision of life in the
spirit of St. Francis of Assisi. It has been one of the
foremost producers of religious broadcast media in the
United States for the past 40 years. Its award-winning
TeleKETICS Division continues to serve the audiovisual
needs of religious educators, liturgists and pastors, while
expanding its ministry into print and publications. Fr.
Anthony Scannell, Capuchin, is President of Franciscan
Communications. For more information, please write to:

Fr. Anthony Scannell, President
1229 S. Santee St.
Los Angeles, CA 90015
(213) 746-2916